Veg

Veg

RECIPES THAT MAKE THE MOST OF ROOTS, BULBS, SHOOTS & STEMS

RYLAND PETERS & SMALL

Senior Designer Megan Smith
Senior Editor Abi Waters
Production Manager Gordana Simakovic
Creative Director Leslie Harrington
Indexer Vanessa Bird

First published in 2026 by
Ryland Peters & Small
20–21 Jockey's Fields,
London WC1R 4BW

www.rylandpeters.com
email: euregulations@
rylandpeters.com

10 9 8 7 6 5 4 3 2 1

Printed in China.

ISBN: 978-1-78879-769-6

MIX
Paper | Supporting responsible forestry
FSC® C106563

A CIP record for this book is available from the British Library. US Library of Congress cataloging-in-Publication Data has been applied for.

The authorised representative in the EEA is Authorised Rep Compliance Ltd., Ground Floor, 71 Lower Baggot Street, Dublin, D02 P593, Ireland
www.arccompliance.com

NOTES

- All spoon measurements are level unless otherwise specified
5 ml = 1 teaspoon
15 ml = 1 tablespoon
- Uncooked or partially cooked eggs should not be served to the very old, frail, young children, pregnant women or those with compromised immune systems.
- When a recipe calls for the grated zest of citrus fruit, buy unwaxed fruit and wash well before using.
- Ovens should be preheated to the specified temperatures.
- To sterilize preserving jars, wash them in hot, soapy water and rinse in boiling water. Place in a large saucepan and cover with hot water. With the saucepan lid on, bring the water to the boil and continue boiling for 15 minutes. Turn off the heat and leave the jars in the hot water until just before they are to be filled. Invert the jars onto a clean dishtowel to dry. Sterilize the lids for 5 minutes, by boiling (remove any rubber seals first). Jars should be filled and sealed while they are still hot.

Contents

The world of veg

There is nothing as satisfying as cooking good produce – homegrown, allotment or farmer's market vegetables used at the height of freshness are more tasty and nutritious than any supermarket offerings. Not only that, but they also cut down on food miles and can be a far more budget-friendly way to eat. Here you'll find a celebration of the bounty you can grow in your garden, allotment or windowbox or even source locally. Home deliveries of mixed veg boxes from local producers are increasingly popular, meaning that you often find yourself with a bunch of veg and no idea or inspiration of what to cook with them.

Discover how to use vegetables creatively in an array of exciting combinations. This book is arranged as an easy reference guide with the recipes for each vegetable grouped together. However, since much of the produce features in combination with other vegetables too, don't forget to check the index for other recipes.

Providing recipes for all your favourite vegetables, this book ensures that there are numerous options for using each vegetable so that you don't have to cook the same dish time and time again in order to use up your produce. And because most seasonal locally-grown vegetables can be picked at their very best, many of the recipes are rustic and unfussy and truly let the flavour of the produce speak for itself.

Growing your own vegetables is immensely satisfying, as is sourcing the best, freshest quality produce from your local farm or supplier. Delve into the vast array of recipes within this collection to ensure you always have a delicious idea to hand to make the most of the vegetables in your kitchen.

Tubers & Roots

POTATOES | SWEET POTATOES | CARROTS | BEETROOT | PARSNIPS | CELERIAC | TURNIPS

Potato & smoky salmon hash

This tasty supper dish featuring hot-smoked salmon flakes is the perfect way to herald the new potato season, bringing the joys of the fresh new potato to the forefront. If you have them to hand, you could also add in 50–75 g/1¾–2¾ oz. smoked salmon pieces and, if liked, this would be extra delicious served with a fried or poached egg on top.

300 g/10½ oz. new potatoes, halved if large
good knob/pat of butter
1 tablespoon olive oil
2 tablespoons salted capers, rinsed and dried
3 spring onions/scallions, chopped
100-g/3½-oz. pack of hot smoked salmon, flaked
1 tablespoon freshly chopped herbs
soured cream and lemon wedges, to serve

SERVES 2

Cook the potatoes in boiling salted water for 10–15 minutes until tender. Drain well and then return to the pan. Gently squash each one with a wooden spoon.

Put the butter, oil and capers in a frying pan/skillet. Turn on the heat and fry until crisp, then set aside on a plate.

Stir in the potatoes and fry for 6–8 minutes until crisp and brown in spots. Add the spring onions, salmon and herbs and toss for a couple of minutes to heat through.

Sprinkle on the crisp capers and serve with a dollop of soured cream and lemon wedges for squeezing.

Warm saffron baby potatoes with lemon & yogurt

This is a lighter way to serve a potato salad that is still creamy but not gloopy or heavy. As the yogurt is swirled through while the potatoes are still warm, it melds well together, or allow to cool and serve as a great side for a barbecue. *Pictured on page 79.*

500 g/1 lb. 2 oz. baby new potatoes
1 tablespoon olive oil
80 g/⅓ cup unsalted butter
1 onion, thinly sliced
pinch of saffron threads
100 g/3½ oz. spinach
2 tablespoons capers
grated zest and juice of 1 lemon
100 g/3½ oz. Greek yogurt
sea salt and black pepper
freshly chopped dill, to garnish

SERVES 4

Put the potatoes in a large saucepan and cover with cold salted water. Bring to the boil, then simmer for 15 minutes until they are tender but still hold their shape. Drain the potatoes and leave them to steam-dry.

Heat the oil with 1 tablespoon of the butter in a large frying pan/skillet over a medium-high heat. Once the butter is foaming, add the onion and saffron and cook for a few minutes, then turn the heat up and add the potatoes and fry for a few more minutes.

Add the remaining butter along with the spinach, capers, lemon zest and juice. Stir everything together for a few minutes so that the potatoes are coated and the spinach has wilted, then season to taste with salt and black pepper. Stir through the Greek yogurt and garnish with dill to serve.

Spiced potatoes in rice pancakes

Potatoes are the perfect vehicle to take on a delicious blend of spices, which are here stuffed into these simple rice pancakes. Similar to Southern India's dosas, the pancake base uses rice and urad dal that are first soaked for a few hours, and then left overnight. As it soaks, it gently ferments, which adds a delicate flavour and a little bubble to the mixture.

300 g/2¼ cups rice flour
100 g/generous ½ cup part urad dal (split black lentils)
1 teaspoon fenugreek seeds
50 g/1¾ oz. ghee
sea salt

SPICED POTATOES
800 g/1¾ lb. potatoes, peeled and cut into 3-cm/1¼-inch pieces
60 ml/¼ cup vegetable oil
1 onion, finely chopped
a thumb-sized piece of fresh ginger, grated
2 garlic cloves, finely chopped
5 fresh curry leaves
1 teaspoon mustard seeds
1 teaspoon ground coriander
1 teaspoon ground turmeric
30 g/1 oz. mixed fresh coriander/cilantro and mint, leaves picked, plus extra to garnish
1 long green chilli/chile, finely chopped
sea salt and black pepper

TO SERVE
grated coconut
sliced green chilli/chile
chilli/chili powder
tamarind chutney
lime wedges

SERVES 4–6

Place the rice flour in a bowl, add just enough cold water to cover and leave to soak for 2–3 hours.

Rinse the urad dal, place in a bowl with enough cold water to cover them and soak for 2–3 hours. Drain the lentils, then place in an electric blender and grind, adding just enough water to form a thick smooth paste.

Mix the lentil paste with the soaked rice flour until you get a thick batter. Add salt to taste and leave the batter in a warm place overnight to ferment.

The next morning, make the spiced potatoes. Cook the potatoes in a saucepan of simmering salted water for 25–30 minutes until tender, then drain well and set aside.

Heat the oil in a large frying pan/skillet, add the onion, ginger, garlic and curry leaves and cook for 7–8 minutes until the onion is soft, then add spices and stir until fragrant. Add potatoes and 80 ml/⅓ cup water, cover and simmer for 3–5 minutes until the flavours have combined and the potatoes are very soft. Stir in the coriander, mint and green chilli and season to taste.

Mix the batter thoroughly again – it should be a thin pancake batter consistency (add water if it's too thick). Add a little ghee to a frying pan until it is hot. Pour a ladleful of the batter into the centre and tilt the pan to spread it until it reaches the edges of the pan. Fry for 2–3 minutes per side, turning once, until golden and crisp. Wipe out the pan with paper towels and repeat with the remaining ghee and batter.

Top the pancakes with the spiced potatoes, coconut, green chilli and chilli powder, garnish with extra coriander and serve with tamarind chutney and lime wedges for squeezing.

Potato & rosemary focaccia

You'll need to start this focaccia 12–18 hours before baking it, but once you use this method you will never go back. It's super bubbly and tasty, and the flavour develops as it slowly proves in the fridge. Once you remove it from the fridge and put it in the pan, leave it untouched until it comes to room temperature. Then you are ready to go and top it with whatever you like – thinly sliced new potatoes work beautifully.

500 g/3½–3⅔ cups strong bread flour
2 teaspoons sea salt
7 g/¼ oz. instant yeast
5 tablespoons olive oil, plus extra for greasing
200 g/7 oz. new potatoes, thinly sliced
3 fresh rosemary sprigs, leaves picked
2 fresh thyme sprigs, leaves picked
flaky sea salt

a 20 x 30-cm/8 x 12-inch baking pan, greased with olive oil

MAKES 1 FOCACCIA LOAF

Start this recipe 12–18 hours before needed.

Mix the flour, salt and yeast well in a bowl. Add 450 ml/scant 2 cups water, then mix well with a spatula to form a dough. Leave the dough in the bowl, slick it with olive oil and cover with cling film/plastic wrap – this is important to prevent it drying out in the fridge.

Place the bowl in the fridge immediately; leave it there to rise for 12–18 hours or up to 3 days. When ready to use, remove from the fridge, knock back/punch down and put in the greased pan.

Don't touch the dough again for 2–4 hours to allow it to come to room temperature slowly (this will depend on how warm your kitchen environment is). It is ready when it feels just warm to the touch, has doubled in size and is nice and 'bubbly'.

Preheat the oven to 200°C/180°C fan/400°F/gas 6.

Pour 2 tablespoons of the olive oil over the dough, and, using your fingers, press straight down to create deep dimples. Sprinkle with flaky sea salt, the sliced potatoes and herbs.

Transfer to the preheated oven immediately and bake for 25 minutes, or until golden all over. Remove the focaccia from the pan and place on a cooling rack to cool completely.

Sweet potato falafel

These baked falafel have a soft finish and a delicate crust rather than the crispness that comes from deep-frying. However, lots of great flavour comes from the fresh and ground herbs and spices, and they are easy to freeze and reheat when the mood strikes. They are delicious served on top of a salad, a grain bowl with a lemon tahini dressing, or in a pita with hummus, slaw and harissa.

2 medium-sized sweet potatoes (about 350 g/12 oz.)
30 g/1 oz. fresh coriander/cilantro leaves and stems
25 g/¾ oz. fresh flat-leaf parsley leaves
2 large spring onions/scallions, roughly chopped
3 garlic cloves
1 teaspoon ground cumin
1 teaspoon ground coriander
¼ teaspoon cayenne pepper
1 teaspoon baking powder
60 g/½ cup chickpea/garbanzo bean (gram) flour
sesame seeds, to sprinkle (optional)
sea salt and black pepper

TAHINI-LEMON DRESSING
50 g/¼ cup tahini, mixed well
60 ml/¼ cup warm water
juice of ½ lemon, plus extra to taste
1 small garlic clove, finely chopped

TO SERVE
diced cucumber
diced tomato
thinly sliced red cabbage
chopped fresh flat-leaf parsley
juice of ½ lemon
pita breads

a baking sheet, greased with a thin layer of olive oil

MAKES 14–16 FALAFEL
TO SERVE 4 PEOPLE

Preheat the oven to 220°C/200°C fan/425°F/gas 7.

Prick the sweet potatoes with a fork a couple of times and place on the oven rack in the preheated oven. Roast for 40–60 minutes, depending on the size of your sweet potatoes, until soft. Remove from the oven and allow to cool. Once cooled, peel off and discard the skin.

Meanwhile, put the coriander, parsley, spring onions and garlic into a small food processor and pulse until everything is finely chopped. Alternatively, you can very finely chop these ingredients with a knife.

In a large bowl, mash the sweet potato flesh with a fork, masher or hand-held mixer until smooth. Season with salt, add the spices, baking powder and chickpea flour and stir vigorously with a rubber spatula or hand-held mixer until everything is well combined. Stir in the herb, onion and garlic mixture until evenly distributed. Let the dough rest in the fridge for about 20 minutes.

Preheat the oven again to 200°C/180°C fan/400°F/gas 6. Scoop out portions of dough with a spoon and then lightly roll into small balls using damp hands to prevent sticking. Go for a size that is somewhere between a ping pong ball and a golf ball. Assemble the falafel on the prepared baking sheet and sprinkle with sesame seeds, if using.

Bake in the preheated oven for 15–20 minutes until golden on the side touching the sheet.

To make the tahini-lemon dressing, combine all the ingredients and a pinch of salt and pepper in a jar with a lid and shake vigorously. Taste for seasoning and add more salt and/or lemon juice if needed.

To serve, combine some diced cucumber, tomato, red cabbage and parsley in a bowl with the fresh lemon juice and a little salt and pepper. Serve the falafel with the cucumber-cabbage salad and tahini-lemon dressing either in a bowl or packed into a pita bread.

Carrot tarte tatin squares with ginger & mint yogurt

When you put glossy, caramelized carrots, soft candied shallots and crisp flaky pastry together, you really can't fail to end up with something very special, and this tatin is certainly that.

1.5 kg/3 lb. 5 oz. carrots
250 g/9 oz. shallots, peeled
3 tablespoons honey
2 tablespoons olive oil
1 tablespoon fresh thyme leaves
30 g/2 tablespoons butter, softened
3 tablespoons light brown muscovado sugar
300 g/10½ oz. ready-made puff pastry
sea salt and black pepper

GINGER & MINT YOGURT

200 g/scant 1 cup natural/plain full-fat yogurt
2-cm/¾-inch piece of fresh ginger, finely grated
1 garlic clove, grated
a small bunch of fresh mint leaves, roughly torn, plus extra to garnish

a 30 x 17-cm/12 x 7-inch brownie pan

MAKES 12 SQUARES

Preheat the oven to 190°C/170°C fan/375°F/gas 5. Cut the carrots into triangular chunks about 2 cm/¾ inch wide at the base. Scatter them over the base of the pan and add the peeled shallots. Mix the honey, olive oil and thyme leaves together and spoon the mixture over the vegetables. Season and roast for about 30 minutes until the carrots have started to soften. Remove the pan from the oven and stir in the butter and sugar.

Roll the pastry out to fit the pan and place it carefully over the vegetables, tucking the edges in.

Bake for about 25 minutes or so, until the pastry is golden and crisp. Remove from the oven and leave to settle for 4–5 minutes, before inverting onto a board and cutting into squares.

Stir the yogurt, grated ginger and grated garlic together in a bowl. Add the torn mint leaves and season with a little salt and freshly ground black pepper. Garnish the carrot tarte tatin with mint leaves and serve with the yogurt in a bowl alongside.

Roasted carrots & legumes with pink peppercorns & parsley

This warming dish perfectly highlights the deep earthy flavour of carrots. It is equally at home as part of a winter menu or served at summer barbecues, so it really is enjoyable at any time of the year. The crispy, popped legumes will capture the hearts of even the least adventurous. If you're cooking for children, maybe grind the pink peppercorns a little to avoid them getting a whole one mid-bite.

6 carrots (or 12 baby carrots)
400-g/14-oz. can chickpeas/garbanzo beans, drained and rinsed
400-g/14-oz. can haricot /navy beans, drained and rinsed
8 garlic cloves (skin-on)
3 tablespoons olive oil
2 teaspoons sea salt
2 teaspoons pink peppercorns
10 g/⅓ oz. fresh flat-leaf parsley, roughly chopped

SERVES 4–6

Preheat the oven to 220°C/200°C fan/425°F/gas 7.

Halve the carrots lengthways (if you're using baby, or just slim carrots, leave whole). Add the prepped carrots, chickpeas, haricot beans, garlic cloves, olive oil, salt and peppercorns to a large roasting pan and toss well to coat. Roast on the top shelf of the preheated oven for 1 hour, turning halfway through cooking.

Once ready, remove from the oven, fold through the parsley and serve.

TIP

- *Swap potatoes (standard and sweet), celeriac and parsnips for carrots. Chickpeas and haricot beans can be swapped for other legumes, such as cannellini beans, but avoid butter/lima beans as they tend to dry out and go chalky.*

Carrot & kale juice

Vegetables can be transformed into delicious tasting, health-giving, brightly coloured juices, and this combination is just the start. Experiment with whichever veg and fruit you have to hand to make your ideal tasting pick-me-up.

200 g/7 oz. carrots, trimmed
2 large bunches of kale
grated zest and juice of 2 oranges

SERVES 4

Add the carrots, kale, orange zest and the juice of 1 of the oranges to a juicer. Process until smooth, adding a little more orange juice as necessary. Serve in tall glasses or transfer to a bottle with a screw-top lid to take out. You may need to give the juice a gentle shake before drinking.

Honeyed heritage carrot & baby beetroot grain platter

A pretty platter of roasted vegetables on a bed of grains to absorb all the juices and finished with tarragon. The pungent, bittersweet flavour of tarragon is often compared to liquorice, anise and fennel, and it really lifts the earthiness of the vegetables. *Pictured on page 22.*

200 g/7 oz. baby beetroot/beet, scrubbed and halved
60 g/¼ cup unsalted butter
60 ml/¼ cup olive oil
300 g/10½ oz. heritage carrots, halved if large
3 garlic cloves, crushed
3 fresh tarragon sprigs
2 fresh thyme sprigs
1 fresh rosemary sprig
½ teaspoon mustard seeds
½ teaspoon cumin seeds
2 tablespoons honey
2 tablespoons apple cider vinegar
100 ml/⅓ cup vegetable stock
200 g/7 oz. cooked grains
sea salt and black pepper
fresh tarragon and flat-leaf parsley, to garnish

SERVES 4

Preheat the oven to 180°C/160°C fan/350°F/gas 4.

Place the baby beetroot on a baking sheet and dot with half the butter and half the olive oil. Season well and roast for 30–40 minutes, or until cooked through.

In a large, deep sauté pan, melt the remaining butter in the olive oil. Add the carrots, garlic, tarragon, thyme, rosemary and mustard and cumin seeds and season with salt and pepper. Cook over a medium heat, stirring occasionally, for about 12 minutes until the carrots are golden. Add the honey and cook, stirring, for about 3 minutes until the honey is lightly caramelized. Stir in the vinegar and cook for about 2 minutes until the carrots are evenly coated. Add the stock, cover and cook over a medium-low heat, stirring occasionally, for about 20 minutes until the carrots are tender and the liquid is syrupy. Transfer the carrots to a plate, discarding the herb sprigs, and leave to cool slightly.

To serve, place the cooked grains on a platter and top with the baby beetroot with their juices, the carrots and their juices and the fresh herbs.

Beetroot risotto

A risotto is a great staple for everyday eating. This simple recipe is particularly tasty and its incredible colour will always be a conversation point too!

- 500 g/1 lb. 2 oz. raw beetroot/beets (about 2 medium–large)
- 2 teaspoons butter
- 2 red onions, finely chopped
- 2 garlic cloves, crushed
- 6–8-cm/2½–3-inch piece of fresh ginger, peeled and grated
- 400 g/2 cups risotto rice, such as Arborio
- 200 ml/¾ cup white wine
- 850 ml/3½ cups vegetable stock
- grated zest and juice of 1–2 lemons
- 50 g/½ cup grated Parmesan
- 3 fresh thyme sprigs, leaves finely chopped
- sea salt and black pepper
- chopped fresh flat-leaf parsley, to garnish

SERVES 4

Preheat the oven to 200°C/180°C fan/400°F/gas 6.

Individually wrap the beetroot in kitchen foil and bake them in the preheated oven for about 40 minutes, or until tender. Set aside until cool enough to handle, then rub off the skins using the foil and cut the beetroot into cubes. Set aside.

Melt the butter in a heavy-based saucepan, add the onions and cook over a low heat for 10 minutes until soft, but not coloured. Add 2 tablespoons water to the pan if the onions are sticking. Stir in the garlic and ginger and cook for 1–2 minutes. Add the rice and cook until it turns opaque. Add the wine and stir until absorbed. Add a quarter of the stock and stir until all the liquid has been absorbed.

Continue to add the stock in stages, stirring constantly until the rice is soft but still has bite. Remove from the heat, then stir in the lemon zest and juice and the Parmesan. Stir in the beetroot and thyme and season with salt and pepper. The consistency should be thick and creamy; add additional stock if required.

Spoon into warmed bowls and top with parsley to serve.

Roasted parsnips, cauliflower, cabbage & fennel with green lentils

This medley really qualifies as roasted veggie heaven – the heat of the oven brings out the natural sweetness of the parsnips in particular and creates the most delicious result.

400 g/14 oz. parsnips, peeled and cut into batons
1 fennel bulb, cut into wedges
6 tablespoons olive oil
3 tablespoons brown rice syrup or maple syrup
1 cauliflower, broken into florets
2 small leeks, trimmed and sliced
1 small pointy cabbage, thickly sliced
1 teaspoon fennel seeds
400-g/14-oz. can green lentils, drained and rinsed
sea salt and black pepper
fresh dill or fennel fronds, to garnish

DRESSING
100 ml/⅓ cup extra virgin olive oil
25 g/1 oz. grain mustard
2 tablespoons cider vinegar
1 tablespoon caster/granulated sugar
grated zest of 1 lemon

SERVES 4

Preheat the oven to 190°C/170°C fan/375°F/gas 5.

Put the parsnip batons and fennel wedges into a large bowl and add half of the oil and the brown rice syrup or maple syrup. Toss to coat everything, and then arrange in a roasting pan. Roast for about 15 minutes until the vegetables are beginning to soften. Add the cauliflower florets to the roasting pan. Scatter the leeks evenly over the top. Cut the cabbage slices into halves or quarters, and lay them here and there over the other veg. Drizzle over the remaining oil, sprinkle with the fennel seeds and season. Return the roasting pan to the oven and roast for a further 20 minutes or so – until the vegetables are soft and slightly charred on the edges.

When the vegetables are cooked, spoon the lentils randomly but evenly over the vegetables and return the roasting pan to the oven for 5 minutes until the lentils are just warmed through.

Meanwhile, whisk all the ingredients for the dressing together in a bowl. Remove the baking sheet from the oven, drizzle the dressing over the vegetables and garnish with dill or fennel fronds.

Maple-roasted celeriac with feta & parsley

Celeriac/celery root is already a fairly sweet vegetable, but the addition of maple syrup here really elevates the flavour in this recipe, and then it's all the better for the added extra of the salty feta. It is just lovely on its own for lunch or serve it with roasted chicken thighs for a wholesome supper dish.

1 celeriac/celery root (about 800 g/1¾ lb.)
4 tablespoons maple syrup
100 g/3½ oz. feta
sea salt and black pepper
olive oil, for roasting
fresh flat-leaf parsley, to garnish
extra virgin olive oil, to serve

SERVES 4

Preheat the oven to 200°C/180°C fan/400°F/gas 6.

Trim the base of the celeriac, then thinly slice down the side of the celeriac with your knife in order to peel the skin (rinse, then freeze the peel and add to your next stock). Cut the celeriac into 2–3-cm/¾–1¼-inch thick wedges and place on a large baking sheet (you may need to use 2 sheets).

Drizzle the maple syrup over the celeriac, following by a good drizzle of olive oil and a very generous scattering of seasoning. Toss to coat and then place on the top shelf of the oven. Let the wedges roast for about 1 hour, turning halfway through, until golden, tender and smelling amazing.

Place them on a serving dish and top with the feta (just crumble it with your hands), then garnish with parsley and serve with a final drizzle of extra virgin olive oil.

Celeriac remoulade

The balance of flavours is the key to this dish. The peppery celeriac/celery root, the nutty oil and the fragrant fennel fronds to finish combine for melt-in-the-mouth perfection.

1 celeriac/celery root
1 quantity of (no egg) mayonnaise (see page 30) or use shop-bought
1 teaspoon English mustard
2–3 dashes of Tabasco sauce
1 bag of rocket/arugula
rapeseed oil, to serve
fresh fennel fronds, to garnish

SERVES 4

Peel the celeriac and carefully chop into matchstick-sized pieces. Mix with the mayonnaise. Add a generous teaspoon of English mustard and a few dashes of Tabasco to taste.

Assemble a handful of rocket on each plate and top with the remoulade. Drizzle with a little rapeseed oil and garnish with fennel fronds.

TIP

- *This creamy remoulade makes a delicious appetizer or side dish and also pairs really well with roasted beetroot/beets.*

Charred turnip salad with (no egg) mayonnaise

Turnips probably don't have the biggest fan club, but when roasted, the transformation is spectacular. This simple salad makes the perfect light lunch or light side dish.

400 g/14 oz. radishes
400 g/14 oz. small turnips, cut into quarters
4 red onions, cut into wedges
1 whole bulb fresh garlic
4 tablespoons olive oil
1 teaspoon caster/granulated sugar
1 tablespoon fresh thyme leaves
150 g/5½ oz. red chicory/endive
fresh dill fronds, to garnish

(NO EGG) MAYONNAISE
2 tablespoons chickpea/garbanzo bean water (aquafaba)
1 scant tablespoon Dijon mustard
2 tablespoons cider vinegar
150 ml/⅔ cup sunflower oil
sea salt

SERVES 4

Preheat the oven to 200°C/180°C fan/400°F/gas 6.

Scatter the radishes, turnips and red onions over a large baking sheet. Cut the whole garlic bulb in half horizontally and lay it in the corner of the baking sheet, cut-sides up.

Drizzle everything with the olive oil. Sprinkle the radishes, turnips and onions with the sugar, but avoid the garlic. Scatter over the thyme leaves. Bake for 35 minutes until the vegetables are soft and golden and slightly charred. Remove from the oven, leave to cool slightly, and transfer to a pretty platter. Arrange the red chicory here and there and garnish with plenty of dill fronds.

For the (no egg) mayonnaise, put the chickpea water, mustard and cider vinegar into a jug and add a pinch of salt. Blitz with a stick blender until mixed. Slowly pour in the sunflower oil while blitzing, until the mixture has emulsified and thickened. Squeeze the roasted garlic out of the crispy little compartments of skin into the mixture and blitz again until well mixed. Serve with the charred turnip and radish salad.

Soupe aux cailloux

Stone soup – a rich vegetable soup – traditionally used a large, clean stone to help break down the vegetables in the days before blenders. You can just use a potato masher instead!

50 g/3½ tablespoons butter
200 g/7 oz. smoked bacon lardons
2 small turnips, finely chopped
1 green cabbage, thinly sliced
2 potatoes, chopped
1 leek, sliced on the diagonal
3 carrots, finely chopped
3 celery sticks/ribs, finely chopped
sea salt and black pepper

2 clean stones (or potato masher)

SERVES 6

Melt the butter in a flameproof casserole and add the bacon. Fry until starting to become golden. Add the vegetables and cook, stirring, until softened. Pour in 1.75 litres/7¾ cups water and season well.

Drop in the stones, if using, and bring to a vigorous simmer. Simmer for 2 hours with the lid on until the stones have broken down the vegetables and you have a rich, thick soup. Alternatively, use a potato masher.

Bulbs, Stems & Stalks

FENNEL | CELERY | LEEKS | ONIONS | ASPARAGUS

Whole baked fennel

Fennel is completely underrated – raw, roasted, barbecued, braised, however it comes. This is a nice, simple, stick-it-in-the-oven recipe that can be a bold side dish or stand-alone meal accompanied by a fresh salad. You can remove the anchovies and omit the Parmesan if you want it to become veggie/vegan, but if you do, add some capers to help with that savoury hit you're losing.

2 whole fennel bulbs
1 vine tomato, thinly sliced
3 anchovy fillets
3 large garlic cloves, thinly sliced
5 g/⅛ oz. fresh oregano, leaves picked
2 tablespoons olive oil
1 tablespoon red wine vinegar
1 lemon, cut into wedges
Parmesan, to serve (optional)
sea salt and black pepper

baking sheet, lined with baking parchment

SERVES 2–4

Preheat the oven to 200°C/180°C fan/400°F/gas 6.

Stand a fennel bulb upright, so it's sitting on its base, then cut a cross down into its heart, without cutting all the way through. Repeat with the second bulb and place on a baking sheet lined with parchment paper. Keep the fennel upright and then stuff with the prepared tomato slices, anchovies (use whole or tear up to spread them out), garlic and oregano. Generously fill the crevices of the fennel bulbs, both the ones made with the knife and the naturally occurring ones as the layers separate towards the tip of the bulbs – this doesn't need to be done neatly!

Drizzle a good glug of olive oil over the stuffed fennel, along with the vinegar and a squeeze of lemon juice too. Season well, then lay the stuffed bulbs on their side, making sure you add the lemon wedges to the tray. Give them one final drizzle of oil over the top, too.

Place on the top shelf of the preheated oven and roast for 45 minutes until caramelized, tender and smelling divine, but not quite ready. Baste the fennel with the pan juices, then return to the oven for a further 45 minutes. Keep an eye on them in the oven and if you're worried about burning, cover them, although the charred bits are delicious.

Once ready, serve the baked fennel sprinkled with a little grated Parmesan, if you like.

TIPS

- *Goes well with barbecued meat or fish and a fresh tomato salad for a great weekend feast.*
- *To make the most of any leftovers you may have, slice the fennel up and turn it into a delicious pasta sauce, with some extra tomatoes and a generous spoonful of mascarpone or crème fraîche or use it to make the pasta bake on page 37.*

Lemon-roasted fennel & dill pasta bake

Fennel and tomato go really well together, so this is a simple combination created to avoid wasting perfectly good leftover baked fennel. Bacon lardons are included here, but you can omit them if preferred.

400 g/14 oz. dried pasta (penne or fusilli work well)
200 g/7 oz. smoked bacon lardons
1 onion, finely chopped
4 garlic cloves, grated
1 tablespoon tomato purée/paste
400 g/14 oz. fresh tomatoes (cherry, vine or plum), roughly chopped
400-g/14-oz. can chopped tomatoes
1 vegetable stock/bouillon cube or stockpot
200–300 g/7–10½ oz. leftover Whole Baked Fennel (see page 34)
sea salt and black pepper
olive oil, for cooking
salad or vegetables, to serve (optional)

TOPPING
5 g/⅛ oz. fresh thyme
50 g/1 cup panko breadcrumbs
3 tablespoons olive oil

30 x 23-cm/12 x 9-inch baking dish

SERVES 4–6

Preheat the oven to 220°C/200°C fan/425°F/gas 7.

Bring a large saucepan of salted water to the boil and cook the pasta according to the package instructions, minus 2 minutes. Drain and rinse the pasta in a colander, then return to the pan (off the heat) and set aside.

Add a drizzle of oil to a wide-bottomed saucepan and, once hot, add the bacon lardons. Fry for 5 minutes until golden. Add the onion to the pan. Cook for 5 minutes, stirring often, until golden, then add the garlic and cook for a minute. Next, add the tomato purée, stir well and cook for 1 minute more.

Add the fresh and canned tomatoes and vegetable stock cube or stock pot to the pan. Fill the empty tomato can one-third full with water and add that too. Bring the sauce to the boil, then reduce the heat and simmer for 10 minutes, stirring often.

Add the leftover baked fennel to the tomato sauce and continue simmering while you prep the topping. Tear the thyme leaves up (removing the thickest stalks) and add to a bowl with the breadcrumbs, oil and a generous pinch of black pepper. Mix well to combine.

When ready, pour the tomato and fennel sauce over the cooked pasta. Mix well to combine, taste to check for seasoning once more and then transfer into the large baking dish.

Sprinkle the topping evenly over the pasta mixture and place on the top shelf in the oven. Bake for 20 minutes until the sauce is bubbling and the topping has crisped up. Serve with salad or vegetables, if liked.

Celery Waldorf

This is a really simple salad, inspired by the classic Waldorf. Celery is often left lurking in the fridge, having been bought for a specific recipe and then never finished, so this is perfect for using up forgotten veg. The salad dressing is a great one for all salads, so keep it in mind for any robust, crunchy leaves or raw veg you want to coat with some flavour.

1 head of celery
150 g/1 cup seedless red grapes
50 g/½ cup walnuts
30 g/¼ cup pumpkin seeds/pepitas
sea salt and black pepper
olive oil, for roasting

DRESSING

2 tablespoons white wine vinegar
1 teaspoon honey
1 tablespoon Dijon mustard
2 tablespoons extra virgin olive oil

SERVES 4–6 AS A SIDE

Preheat the oven to 220°C/200°C fan/425°F/gas 7.

Pull off any celery leaves (leaving them whole) and add to a large salad bowl. Thinly slice the whole celery at an angle. Scatter a third of the sliced celery on a baking sheet, drizzle with oil and a pinch of seasoning and roast on the top shelf of the preheated oven for about 20 minutes until lightly caramelized and tender. Add the remaining sliced celery to the salad bowl.

While the celery roasts, thinly slice the grapes as best you can (a small serrated knife is best). They don't need to be really thin, but try to cut each grape into 3 or 4 slices.

Add the grapes to the salad bowl, along with all of the dressing ingredients, then toss really well. While this method means less dishwashing, it does mean you need to mix the salad and liquids thoroughly so that they combine and emulsify. So, hands in and a minute or two of gently tossing and turning.

When the roasted celery is done, add the walnuts and pumpkin seeds to the baking sheet, toss to coat in the existing oils and return to the oven for a final 5 minutes. Once ready, give them a final jiggle, then add to the salad bowl and mix to combine everything. You'll have a crunchy but warm, tart yet sweet, gentle but bold salad ready for you, right there.

TIPS

- *This salad is delicious with chicken thighs, or try it with crackers, salami and cheese for a take on a traditional ploughman's lunch.*
- *It is also brilliant piled into a sandwich or toastie with some ham and cheese, or even better, rare roast beef left over from your Sunday roast.*

Leek & cauliflower gratin

Cheesy leeks and cauliflower cheese have got to be some of the most comforting side dishes ever. This combination of the two uses pre-roasted veg to give it more depth of flavour and has a herby, garlicky, crunchy topping for added flair. Add extras into the mix, if you like – more greens, cooked potatoes, some leftover pasta, cooked meats such as bacon, chorizo, chicken, whatever you like really.

3 leeks
1 cauliflower head
50 g/3½ tablespoons butter
50 g/heaped ⅓ cup plain/all-purpose flour
700 ml/3 cups whole milk
200 g/7 oz. Cheddar cheese (or a mix of whatever you have in the fridge), grated
5 g/⅛ oz. fresh oregano leaves
5 g/⅛ oz. fresh sage leaves
40 g/¾ cup breadcrumbs
10 cloves of roasted confit garlic (usually sold in jars) (optional)
sea salt and black pepper
olive oil, for roasting

SERVES 4–6

Preheat the oven to 220°C/200°C fan/425°F/gas 7.

Trim, rinse, then slice the leeks into 6-cm/2½-inch chunks. Tear the leaves off the cauliflower (but don't throw them away), cut the head of the cauliflower into medium florets and chop the stalk into chunks. Add them all (including the leaves and stalk) to your largest baking sheet and drizzle with a glug of olive oil and a good pinch of seasoning. Toss to coat, then place on the top shelf of the preheated oven to roast for 30 minutes.

Meanwhile, make your sauce. Add the butter to a medium saucepan set over a medium heat and let melt. Once gently sizzling, add the flour and mix vigorously to combine. Let this roux 'cook out' for about 3–4 minutes until it becomes a 'brown roux' (you want it a nice shade of butterscotch), then add a first splash of the milk and whisk. This will cause it to thicken.

Once that milk has all been absorbed and become stiff, add another glug of milk, and continue to do so, gradually, whisking continuously. Once all the milk is in the pan, it's time to just stand there and gently stir until the sauce thickens. It'll take about 5 minutes or so. When your sauce has a lovely, custard-like thickness, remove from the heat and fold through three-quarters of the grated cheese. Taste to check for seasoning, you'll probably need to add more salt and pepper. When you're happy with the flavour, set aside until the veg is roasted and out of the oven.

Meanwhile, mix the remaining grated cheese with the herbs, breadcrumbs and a pinch more seasoning. This is your topping.

Remove the baking sheet from the oven, transfer the roasted veg to a baking dish and then pour all of the cheese sauce on top. Sprinkle over the topping, then finish with the confit garlic cloves, if using – just dot them on top randomly. Bake the gratin on the top shelf of the preheated oven for 25 minutes until golden brown, bubbling and crisp.

Leek, cauliflower & fennel soup

Creamy and flavourful, this soup is a cosy winter favourite. The colour of the soup can feel a little drab, so toss in a couple of handfuls of spinach at the end to brighten it up.

1 head of cauliflower, cut into florets
1 large bulb of fennel, sliced into 1.5-cm/½-inch thick pieces, long green stems and fronds cut off and set aside for garnishing
olive or avocado oil, for frying
1 leek, thinly sliced into half-moons
3 garlic cloves, finely chopped
1½ teaspoons fresh thyme leaves
950 ml/4 cups vegetable stock
2 handfuls of baby spinach (optional)
sea salt and black pepper
lemon wedges and good-quality bread, to serve

2 baking sheets, greased

SERVES 4

Preheat the oven to 200°C/180°C fan/400°F/gas 6. Scatter the cauliflower and fennel onto the greased baking sheets. Season with salt and roast for 20–25 minutes until both vegetables are golden and tender.

Meanwhile, in a large saucepan, heat enough oil to cover the base over a medium heat. Add the sliced leek and a pinch of salt and cook for about 10 minutes, stirring occasionally, until softened and starting to turn golden. Stir in the garlic and cook for another minute. Add the thyme leaves and let it sizzle for 30 seconds.

Stir in the roasted cauliflower and fennel, followed by the vegetable stock. Turn up the heat to bring to a boil, then reduce the heat and simmer for about 5 minutes. If you're adding spinach, stir it in now and allow to wilt. Remove from the heat and allow to cool for 5 minutes.

Blend the soup with a handheld stick blender until smooth. Pour into bowls and serve with lemon wedges for squeezing over, ground black pepper and good bread. Garnish with the reserved fennel fronds, if you like.

Charred leeks with tarator sauce

Barbecued leeks topped with a nutty sauce is a Middle Eastern favourite. This recipe uses macadamias, although traditionally it is prepared with ground almonds or walnuts.

750 g/1 lb. 10 oz. baby leeks
2–3 tablespoons olive oil
sea salt and black pepper

TARATOR SAUCE

50 g/⅓ cup macadamia nuts, toasted
25 g/½ cup fresh breadcrumbs
2 garlic cloves, crushed
100 ml/⅓ cup extra virgin olive oil
1 tablespoon lemon juice
2 tablespoons boiling water

SERVES 4

To make the sauce, put the nuts into a food processor and grind coarsely, then add the breadcrumbs, garlic, salt and pepper and process again to form a smooth paste. Transfer to a bowl and very gradually whisk in the olive oil, lemon juice and the boiling water to form a sauce. Season to taste with salt and pepper.

Preheat the barbecue. Trim the leeks and brush them with a little olive oil. Season with salt and cook over medium hot coals for 6–10 minutes, turning occasionally, until charred and tender. Transfer to a serving plate, sprinkle with olive oil, then pour the sauce over the top and serve.

Roasted shallots with green yogurt

Keeping the skin on gives the shallots (and all alliums) a natural jacket, letting the layers soften and caramelize, while protecting the delicate flesh from burning or drying out. It also means the prep is minimal and that the edible part (all but the outer layers of brittle skin) almost gets braised in its own juices. Glorious. Serve the roasted shallots with the quickest sauce ever – all it calls for is some leftover pesto, chimichurri or salsa and natural/plain yogurt for a delicious finishing touch.

6–8 shallots (skin on)
60 g/2¼ oz. herb-based cold sauce such as pesto, salsa or chimichurri
80 g/3 oz. natural/plain yogurt
sea salt and black pepper
olive oil, for roasting

SERVES 4–6

Preheat the oven to 200°C/180°C fan/400°F/gas 6.

Halve the shallots lengthways and add them all to a large baking sheet. Drizzle over some olive oil and season well. Toss to coat the shallots and then place on the top shelf of the oven and roast for 40 minutes.

Mix the herb sauce and yogurt in a small bowl with a pinch of salt and pepper (taste to check for seasoning).

When the shallots are done, let them sit for 5 minutes, then transfer to a serving dish and spoon over the green yogurt. Pass around some napkins and encourage people to enjoy with their hands, like mussels!

Caramelized red onion chutney

This chutney is a balance of sweet and sour flavours and the lovely depth you get from the red onions. Adding a hint of spice with the chilli/chile will get your taste buds working.

2 kg/4½ lb. red onions
500 ml/2 cups balsamic vinegar
250 ml/1 cup sherry vinegar
200 ml/¾ cup red wine
500 g/1 lb. 2 oz. green apples, cored and diced into 5-mm/¼-inch cubes (skin on)
100 g/⅔ cup sultanas/golden raisins
150 g/¾ cup brown sugar
½ teaspoon ground cinnamon
1 teaspoon ground ginger
1 small red chilli/chile, thinly sliced
2 teaspoons table salt

MAKES ABOUT 2 KG/4½ LB.

Thinly slice the onions using a food processor. Chop them again using a knife, into thin, irregular pieces.

Put all of the ingredients in a large saucepan and set over a medium heat. Bring the mixture to a low simmer and cover. Allow it to simmer gently for 1½ hours, stirring occasionally, to cook everything thoroughly.

Take the lid off and turn up the heat to a rapid simmer. Reduce the liquid until it is about one-third of the previous quantity and has thickened to the consistency of double/heavy cream.

Spoon carefully into sterilized glass jars. Seal and leave to finish cooling in the jars. Store for up to 6 months and, once opened, store in the fridge and use within 4 weeks.

Asparagus & gorgonzola frittata

Traditionally, a frittata has a potato base, but this recipe simply uses in-season asparagus, eggs, herbs and spring onions/scallions, finished with gorgonzola. If asparagus is out of season, courgettes/zucchini are a great alternative.

small knob/pat of butter
1 shallot, finely chopped
4 spring onions/scallions, finely chopped
200 g/7 oz. asparagus (use a mix of green and wild asparagus if you can find them), woody ends snapped off
6 eggs, beaten
grated zest of 1 lemon
100 g/3½ oz. gorgonzola, crumbled
sea salt and black pepper
salad leaves, to serve

SERVES 2

Heat the butter in a small frying pan/skillet over a low heat. Add the shallot and spring onions and cook gently for about 8 minutes until soft and translucent, stirring to stop them catching. Add the asparagus and cook for 3 minutes, stirring.

Preheat the grill/broiler.

Pour the eggs into the pan, sprinkle over the lemon zest and season with salt and pepper. Cook until almost set, without stirring. Sprinkle over the cheese and pop under the grill until just set and the cheese is melted and golden. Leave to cool slightly and serve warm, cut into wedges, with a green salad.

Asparagus with hollandaise sauce

Asparagus and freshly made lemony hollandaise is a real treat. Griddling asparagus gives it smokiness and bite; and makes a much more flavourful dish than boiled asparagus.

250 g/2 sticks unsalted butter
4 egg yolks
grated zest and juice of 1 lemon
20 asparagus spears, woody ends snapped off
vegetable oil, to coat
sea salt and ground white pepper

SERVES 4

To make the hollandaise sauce, melt the butter in a saucepan set over a medium heat. Allow it to bubble for a few minutes to cook off the water. Set aside until it is just cool enough to touch.

Put the egg yolks, lemon juice and a pinch of salt and pepper into a jug/pitcher. Slowly place a handheld stick blender into the jug, capturing the yolks under the blade. While continuously blending, pour the melted butter in, taking about 30 seconds, then slowly pull the blender out to combine the butter and yolks. This will form a sauce; it really is that simple.

Lightly oil and season the asparagus with a little salt. Preheat a griddle/grill pan over a medium–high heat. Carefully place the asparagus spears in the pan and cook until they are just starting to blacken, turn over and repeat.

Serve simply on a warm plate with a generous dollop of hollandaise sauce, topped with a sprinkle of lemon zest and ground white pepper.

Risotto primavera

This recipe is an invitation to improvise. This simplified method of making risotto requires less stirring, because you keep the pan covered for the first 12 minutes. Cook or prepare the vegetables of your choice separately, and stir them in for the last 6–8 minutes. If you or your dinner companion enjoys a touch of heat, add a good pinch of crushed chillies/hot pepper flakes along with the stock. As always, leave the risotto for a few minutes at the end before serving, so the flavours can get to know one another.

1 tablespoon olive oil
1 small onion, chopped
100 g/generous ½ cup risotto rice
450 ml/scant 2 cups hot vegetable stock or chicken stock
4 tablespoons freshly grated Parmesan, plus extra to serve
good knob/pat of butter
squeeze of lemon juice

VEGETABLES
150 g/2¼ cups button mushrooms, trimmed and pan-fried for 5 minutes
150 g/5¼ oz. asparagus, or green/French beans, trimmed, cut into bite-size pieces and boiled for 3–5 minutes until tender
handful of frozen peas (no need to defrost)

SERVES 2

Heat the oil in a medium pan, one with a lid, and fry the onion for 2–3 minutes until translucent but not brown. Stir in the rice and cook for a similar time until the grains are translucent. Add about three-quarters of the stock and season, bring to a gentle simmer and cover with the lid. Cook for 12 minutes, reducing the heat as necessary to ensure a slow but constant simmer, and stirring once or twice.

Stir in the prepared vegetables and simmer on, uncovered, stirring frequently this time, for another 6–8 minutes until everything is hot and the rice cooked.

Set aside for 3–4 minutes, then stir in the Parmesan, butter and lemon juice. Serve in warmed bowls with extra Parmesan.

TIP

- *It can be spring any time you fancy – just add whatever vegetables come to hand, fresh, jarred or frozen. Stir in halved cherry tomatoes at the end, or marinated artichoke hearts, roughly chopped, or other antipasti vegetables such as (bell) peppers or mushrooms, or any vegetables from the freezer.*

Fruiting Vegetables

AUBERGINES | PEPPERS | TOMATOES | CUCUMBERS | SWEETCORN | ARTICHOKES

Ratatouille tart with mascarpone, mozzarella & basil

A perfect tart to serve to friends. It can be eaten warm or at room temperature, so can sit until you are ready to eat. This goes well alongside a charcuterie board and a crisp salad. Best eaten on the day of making.

1 aubergine/eggplant, cut into 5-mm/¼-inch slices
2 courgettes /zucchini, cut into 5-mm/¼-inch slices
3 tablespoons olive oil, plus extra to serve
3 large tomatoes (a mixture of different colours looks nice), cut into 5-mm/¼-inch slices
320-g/11½-oz. sheet of ready-rolled puff pastry
4 tablespoons mascarpone
100 g/3½ oz. roasted red (bell) peppers from a jar, sliced
2 mozzarella balls, sliced
1 egg, beaten
sea salt and black pepper
plain/all-purpose flour, for dusting
fresh basil leaves, to garnish

SERVES 4–6

Preheat the oven to 240°C/220°C fan/475°F/gas 9.

Lay the aubergine and courgette slices out on a couple of large baking sheets and brush them on both sides with 2 tablespoons of the olive oil. Season, roast in the preheated oven for 10 minutes until starting to soften, then leave to cool for 10 minutes. Meanwhile, pat the tomato slices dry and leave to drain on paper towels.

Put a large baking sheet on the top shelf of the oven to heat up. Unroll the puff pastry sheet on a floured work surface and roll out further in one direction to make a square about 3 mm/⅛ inch thick, then trim off the corners to make a 30-cm/12-inch round disc. Transfer the pastry circle to a large piece of non-stick baking paper so that it's easier to move once it's assembled.

Spread the mascarpone over the centre of the pastry, leaving a 5-cm/2-inch border all round the edge, and season with salt and pepper. Arrange the courgette, aubergine, tomato, red pepper and mozzarella slices on top of the mascarpone in a spiral or concentric circles.

Drizzle with the remaining oil and fold in the sides to overlap the filling slightly, making a 3–4-cm/1½–1¾-inch wide crust. Brush the crust with egg, sprinkle with a little salt and slide the tart, on its paper, onto the hot baking sheet in the oven.

Bake for 20–25 minutes until the pastry is puffed and golden and the vegetables have softened. Leave to rest for at least 20 minutes.

Serve warm or at room temperature, scattered with basil and drizzled with more oil.

Roasted aubergine po' boys with white bean purée & herby slaw

These po' boys are a plant-based ode to New Orleans' old-school charm and its new wave of creative cuisine. The aubergine/eggplant slices act like a sponge, perfectly taking on the punchy Cajun spices and oil. The softened Cajun aubergine is then used to create these fabulous baguettes with the perfect combo of spicy veg, creamy beans and herby slaw.

- 1 large aubergine/eggplant, sliced into thick rounds
- 1–2 tablespoons Cajun spice mix
- avocado or olive oil, for brushing

WHITE BEAN PURÉE

- 160 g/1¼ cups canned white beans, drained and rinsed
- 1 tablespoon tahini
- 1 tablespoon lemon juice
- ½ garlic clove
- ¼ teaspoon chilli flakes/hot red pepper flakes
- ⅛ teaspoon smoked paprika
- 1–2 tablespoons iced water (optional)
- sea salt

HERBY SLAW

- 60 g/1 cup thinly sliced red cabbage
- 20 g/¾ oz. fresh flat-leaf parsley or coriander/cilantro leaves (or a mixture), finely chopped
- ½ garlic clove, finely grated
- 1 tablespoon olive oil
- 2 teaspoons red wine vinegar

TO SERVE

- fresh baguettes, cut into 15-cm/6-inch lengths and split in half

baking sheet, lined

MAKES 2–3 BIG SANDWICHES OR 4 SMALLER ONES

Preheat the oven to 200°C/180°C fan/400°F/gas 6.

Brush the aubergine slices on both sides with oil and spread out on the lined baking sheet. Sprinkle with a little of the Cajun spice mix to give a light coating.

Roast in the preheated oven for about 15 minutes. Flip the aubergine slices over and sprinkle the other side with Cajun spice mix. Bake for a further 10 minutes until soft and golden.

To make the white bean purée, combine all the ingredients in a food processor or blender and purée until smooth. Add the iced water for a smoother consistency if preferred.

Combine the slaw ingredients in a bowl and season to taste with salt.

Assemble the sandwiches with a good slathering of white bean purée on the baguettes, topped with the aubergine slices and herby slaw.

Pickled aubergine

Not your run-of-the-mill pickled veg, but one not to be missed if you have a glut.

- 250 ml/1 cup white wine vinegar
- 1 aubergine/eggplant, chopped
- 1 large red chilli/chile, sliced
- 1 garlic clove, sliced
- ½ teaspoon caraway seeds
- 3 tablespoons olive oil

MAKES 375 ML/1½ CUPS

Put the vinegar in a small saucepan with 500 ml/2 cups water and bring to the boil. Add the aubergine, cover with a lid and turn off the heat. Let the aubergine sit in the liquid for about 20 minutes. Drain well and let the aubergine cool completely. Put the aubergine in a bowl with the chilli, garlic, caraway seeds and oil. Cover and refrigerate for 1 day before eating.

Caponata facile e veloce

Caponata is one of Sicily's many contributions to Italian cookery, and it can be made many ways. This 'quick and easy' version is colourful and satisfying, and can be served with bread, couscous or pasta – hot, warm or cold. Take a little trouble in step 3 to make sure the dish is well seasoned, to bring out all the rich flavours.

1 tablespoon olive oil, plus a little extra
1 onion, chopped
1 aubergine/eggplant, cut into 1-cm/½-inch cubes
1 garlic clove, crushed
1 teaspoon dried oregano
pinch of crushed chillies/hot red pepper flakes
400-g/14-oz. can cherry tomatoes
200 ml/¾ cup wine or water
2 tablespoons capers (if using salted, rinse)
12 pitted black or green olives, halved
1 tablespoon raisins or sultanas/golden raisins, chopped (optional)
squeeze of lemon juice
2 squares of dark/bittersweet chocolate (optional)
pinch of sugar (optional)
2 tablespoons flaked/slivered almonds, toasted
sea salt and black pepper
bread, to serve (optional)

SERVES 2

Heat the oil in a shallow saucepan. Add the onion and aubergine and fry for 10 minutes until softened and golden. Add the garlic, oregano and crushed chillies and cook for 30 seconds, then add the tomatoes, wine, capers, olives and raisins (if using).

Simmer, uncovered, for 5–10 minutes until slightly thickened.

To finish, stir in the lemon juice and season generously. Melt in the chocolate, if using, and taste again. If necessary, add a pinch of sugar to sweeten before sprinkling over the flaked almonds and serving with bread, if liked.

Honey, miso & soy aubergines, with yogurt & coriander

The key to this dish is cooking the aubergines/eggplants for a long time. The dish is rich and punchy so pairs well with a refreshing leafy salad on the side.

4 aubergines/eggplants
4 tablespoons runny honey
100 g/6 tablespoons red miso paste
3 tablespoons soy sauce
3 tablespoons vegetable oil
300 g/1⅓ cups natural/plain yogurt
30 g/1 oz. freshly coriander/ cilantro, chopped
1 red chilli/chile, thinly sliced
30 g/1 oz. crispy onions
1 teaspoon pul biber
sea salt and black pepper

baking sheet, lined

SERVES 4–6

Preheat the oven to 200°C/180°C fan/400°F/gas 6.

Quarter the aubergines lengthways and put onto the lined baking sheet. Add the honey, miso paste, soy sauce and vegetable oil to a bowl with some black pepper and mix with a fork to combine, then pour liberally over the aubergines and rub into the wedges with your hands.

Place the dressed aubergines on the top shelf of the preheated oven and bake for 1 hour, turning and basting 3 times. If the aubergines colour too much, cover with an upside-down baking sheet. You want them to get a deep caramelization though, so fear not.

Meanwhile, season the yogurt with a pinch of salt and pepper and spread over a large serving dish.

Once the aubergines are very soft, sticky and well-coloured, transfer to the serving dish in a pile on top of the yogurt, top with the coriander, crispy onions and fresh chilli, finishing with the pul biber. Make sure you spoon over any remaining roasting sauce onto the dish as well.

Aubergine pasta with green beans

This dish is vibrant and colourful with surprising and tasty flavours. From nutty aubergine/eggplant pasta to creamy feta cheese, this dish is fun to make and to eat.

1 large aubergine/eggplant, peeled and very thinly sliced into ribbons
2 red onions, finely diced
50 g/⅓ cup pine nuts
200 g/2 cups green/French beans
grated zest and juice of ½ lemon
vegetable oil, for frying
100 g/¾ cup feta cheese
sea salt

SERVES 4

Pour enough oil to cover the bottom of a large, heavy-based saucepan. Set over a medium heat and, when the pan is hot enough, add the aubergine ribbons and turn them quickly while they cook to coat them with oil. Add the onions and pine nuts. Cook for a few minutes, turning frequently until the onions are starting to turn golden. Add a couple of pinches of salt and turn again before adding the trimmed beans.

Cook for a further 2 minutes to heat the beans through, then squeeze the lemon juice over the pan and add the zest. Serve with the feta crumbled over the top.

Red pepper, chorizo & new potato frittata

A frittata (Italian) is started on the hob/stovetop and finished in the oven, whereas a tortilla (Spanish) is cooked entirely on the hob. This flavoursome dish combines the best of both.

1 tablespoon olive oil
150–200 g/5¼–7 oz. baby new potatoes, scrubbed and halved
50 g/1¾ oz. cured chorizo, cut into thin semi-circles
4 eggs, any size
4 tablespoons double/heavy cream
2 teaspoons plain/all-purpose flour
1 teaspoon smoked paprika
75–100 g/¾–1 cup grated Cheddar, plus a little extra to finish
small bunch of fresh basil, roughly chopped
20 g/1½ tablespoons butter
80 g/3 oz. roasted red (bell) peppers, sliced
sea salt and black pepper

SERVES 2

Heat the oil in a frying pan/skillet (one with a lid) and fry the potatoes with a little seasoning, covered, for 20–25 minutes until golden and tender, shaking the pan occasionally. (If more convenient, you can do this in a small roasting pan at 200°C/180°C fan/400°F/gas 6 for 25–30 minutes.) Add the chorizo for the last couple of minutes, then remove to a heatproof bowl with a slotted spoon (no need to wash the pan).

Preheat the oven to 190°C/170°C fan/375°F/gas 5.

Mix the eggs, cream, flour, paprika, cheese and basil in a bowl with a good amount of seasoning.

Heat the butter in the same frying pan until the foam has died down, then pour in the egg mixture. After a minute, lift the edge (as if making an omelette) to let the uncooked egg flow underneath. When there is no more uncooked egg, scatter the potato mixture and red peppers over. Lower the heat and cook, covered, for 2–3 minutes, until you can look underneath and see (and smell) that the base has browned.

Scatter with a little extra cheese and bake, uncovered, for 4–8 minutes until golden and beginning to puff. Remove from the oven, leave in the pan for a minute, then cut into slices and slide onto plates to serve.

Chipotle red pepper soup

While this is a fantastic summer soup, it can be made all year round. On hot days, serve this soup fridge cold, like a Spanish gazpacho.

4 red (bell) peppers
2 tablespoons olive oil
knob/pat of butter
2 large brown onions, sliced
3 garlic cloves, thinly sliced
1 tablespoon smoked paprika
1 teaspoon ground coriander
1 tablespoon chipotle paste, thinly sliced
350 g/12 oz. tomatoes
400 ml/1¾ cups vegetable stock, chicken stock or water
1 teaspoon light brown muscovado sugar
sea salt and black pepper
fresh basil, to garnish
extra virgin olive oil, to serve

SERVES 4

Preheat the oven to 240°C/220°C fan/450°F/gas 8.

Discard the (bell) pepper stalk (leave the pith and seeds) and chop into 3–4-cm/1¼–1½-inch pieces. Add to a large baking sheet, drizzle with the olive oil, season generously and toss to coat. Place on the top shelf of the oven and roast for 20 minutes until tender and lightly charred.

Meanwhile, melt the butter in a large flameproof casserole dish or saucepan. When gently sizzling, add the onion. Gently fry for 15 minutes until soft and lightly caramelized. Add the garlic, spices and chipotle paste to the pan and fry for 2 minutes until fragrant. Add the tomatoes, stock, sugar and the roasted veg (if they're not ready, just add them later).

Bring to the boil, then reduce the heat to a very gentle simmer and cook for 10 minutes. Remove the pan from the heat, then blitz the soup using an handheld stick blender. Taste to check for seasoning and add more salt, pepper and chipotle paste to your liking. Divide into bowls, garnish with fresh basil and serve with a drizzle of extra virgin olive oil.

Pepper, tomato & celery juice

This recipe has more than a nod to a Bloody Mary cocktail. Adding a generous glug of tequila makes a perfect pre-dinner drink, too.

2 red (bell) peppers
8 large tomatoes, roughly chopped
4 celery sticks, thinly sliced, tops reserved for garnishing
2 tablespoons runny honey
a generous splash of smoked chipotle Tabasco sauce
juice of ½ lemon
lemon wedges, to serve

SERVES 4

Over a naked flame, or in a very hot oven at 240°C/220°C fan/475°F/gas 9, carefully blacken the outer skin of the peppers for 3–4 minutes, then brush away any loose bits of blackened skin.

Put the tomatoes, blackened peppers, celery, honey, smoked chipotle Tabasco sauce and lemon juice into a juicer and pulse to combine.

Pour the juice into glasses and serve immediately dressed with a few celery leaves and a wedge of lemon for squeezing.

Blackened Romano pepper, tomato & chilli salad

This recipe works well on the hob/stovetop, but is particularly great if you can char the peppers on a barbecue/outdoor grill. It takes the same amount of time as in a frying pan/skillet, so no edits or time needed for either method. There's some chopping to do, but settle in and practise your knife skills, mix it all up and serve!

4 Romano peppers
200 g/7 oz. tomatoes, finely chopped
1 green chilli/chile, deseeded and finely chopped
10 g/⅓ oz. fresh flat-leaf parsley, chopped
10 g/⅓ oz. fresh coriander/cilantro, chopped
1 tablespoon pomegranate molasses
1 teaspoon good-quality balsamic vinegar
1 teaspoon olive oil
sea salt and black pepper

SERVES 4

Turn the barbecue/outdoor grill on if you're using it. If not, heat a large, dry frying pan/skillet on a high heat (no oil).

Pierce the Romano peppers a few times to allow steam to escape freely during cooking.

Add the Romano peppers to the hot barbecue or frying pan and char on a high heat for 15 minutes until well blackened, but not necessarily tender. They don't need to be really soft, so focus on charring, over the cooking. Once you are happy with the peppers, remove from the heat and set aside to cool.

Add the tomatoes, chilli, herbs, molasses, vinegar, olive oil and some seasoning to a bowl and set aside.

Remove the stalks and seeds from the Romano peppers then finely chop the flesh. Add it to the bowl, then mix well to combine. Taste to check for seasoning and then serve.

TIPS

- *You can use (bell) peppers instead of Romano and any tomatoes are fine here. Swap in balsamic glaze instead of molasses and any vinegar you like, but red wine vinegar probably works the best.*
- *Serve cold with literally anything, fold into a pasta sauce or ragù or use as a relish-type addition to a sandwich.*

Simple summer tomato sauce

There is nothing more satisfying than making your own tomato sauce. This sauce combines the velvety base of bought passata/strained tomatoes, adding in cherry tomatoes as well as other flavour enhancers. The addition of the cherry tomatoes makes it a perfect simple summer tomato sauce that can be used in so many dishes.

100 ml/⅓ cup extra virgin olive oil
1 onion, finely chopped
3 garlic cloves, crushed
500 g/1 lb. 2 oz. cherry tomatoes, halved
800 ml/3⅓ cups passata/ strained tomatoes
1 teaspoon dried oregano
pinch of sugar
30 g/1 oz. fresh basil leaves, torn
sea salt and black pepper

sterilized glass jars

MAKES 2–3 JARS

Stir the oil, onion and garlic together in a large saucepan over a low heat until golden. Add the tomatoes, season to taste and continue to cook, stirring occasionally, until falling apart. Add the passata, oregano and sugar and simmer for about 30 minutes until thickened. Remove from the heat and stir in the basil. Decant into sterilized jars (see page 4).

The sauce will keep in the refrigerator for 1 week. Alternatively, freeze in batches and you will have a lovely fresh tomato sauce to hand whenever you need it.

Summer tomato tart

Gloriously simple to make, this Mediterranean-flavoured tart tastes as good as it looks. If available, use different coloured tomatoes for the topping for extra visual appeal. *Pictured on page 69.*

300 g/10½ oz. puff pastry dough
2 tablespoons black olive tapenade
400 g/14 oz. ripe tomatoes, cut into 5-mm/⅛-inch thick slices
sea salt and black pepper
plain/all-purpose flour, for dusting
fresh basil leaves, to garnish

baking sheet, greased

SERVES 6

On a lightly floured surface, thinly roll out the puff pastry to form a circle about 27 cm/11 inch in diameter. Chill the pastry circle in the fridge for 30 minutes.

Preheat the oven to 200°C/180°C fan/400°F/gas 6.

Place the chilled pastry circle on the greased baking sheet. Spread the olive tapenade evenly over the pastry, leaving a 2-cm/¾-inch rim around the edge. Arrange the tomato slices in spiralling rings over the tapenade, overlapping them slightly. Season with a little salt and pepper, bearing in mind the saltiness of the tapenade.

Bake in the preheated oven for 40 minutes, then reduce the oven temperature to 150°C/130°C fan/300°F/gas 2 and bake for a further 1 hour until the pastry is crisp and golden-brown and the tomatoes are cooked through. Serve warm or at room temperature, garnished with basil.

Shakshuka

This North African dish is a great choice for two, because for larger numbers it's difficult to fit the eggs in the pan. It makes a satisfying supper served with pita bread, other flatbreads or crusty French bread.

Zhoug (pronounced 'zoog') is a spicy coriander-/cilantro-based sauce originally from Yemen, but popular throughout the Middle East; it adds excitement to falafels, roasted veg, wraps and pitas. You can make it yourself by blitzing fresh coriander and parsley with chillies/chiles and a little cardamom and cumin, but bought in small jars, it is a handy condiment to keep in the fridge.

1 tablespoon olive oil
1 small onion, chopped
½ small red chilli/chile, deseeded and finely chopped
1 garlic clove, sliced
squeeze of tomato purée/paste
400-g/14-oz. can cherry tomatoes
4 tablespoons chargrilled red (bell) peppers from a jar, sliced (optional)
½ teaspoon sugar
1 teaspoon smoked paprika
½ teaspoon ground cumin
4 eggs, any size
sea salt and black pepper

TO SERVE (OPTIONAL)
crumbled feta
sliced pitted black olives
zhoug
bread

SERVES 2

Heat the oil in a large frying pan/skillet, one with a lid, and cook the onion, chilli and garlic for 5 minutes until softened. Add the tomato purée for 30 seconds, then the tomatoes, peppers, sugar, spices, 100 ml/⅓ cup water (you can use the can as a measure) and season with salt and pepper. Simmer, uncovered, for 8–10 minutes until thickened and then check the seasoning.

Make 4 indentations in the surface of the sauce. Break an egg into a small dish and slide into the first indentation, then repeat with the other 3 eggs. Sprinkle salt and pepper over the eggs, then spoon some of the sauce over the whites (which will spread), but leave the yolks uncovered. Cook over a low heat, covered, for 6–8 minutes until the eggs are how you like them.

Lift out the eggs with a spatula and spoon the sauce around them. Top with crumbled feta and olives, if using, and flick over some zhoug, if you wish. Serve with some good bread.

Greek rice-stuffed tomatoes

Evoke summer holidays on Greek islands with this Mediterranean dish, in which a few simple ingredients are transformed into a tasty and satisfying meal.

4–6 large tomatoes
3 tablespoons olive oil
1 small onion, finely chopped
150 g/¾ cup long-grain rice, rinsed
1 teaspoon tomato purée/paste
2 tablespoons chopped fresh flat-leaf parsley
2 tablespoons chopped fresh dill
2 tablespoons chopped fresh mint
1 teaspoon grated lemon zest
sea salt and black pepper

SERVES 4

Preheat the oven to 200°C/180°C fan/400°F/gas 6.

Cut the tops off the tomatoes and carefully scoop out and reserve the soft pulp. Put the tomato shells in a baking dish large enough to hold all the tomatoes upright. Set aside with the caps until ready to bake.

Heat 2 tablespoons of the oil in a frying pan/skillet set over a low heat. Add the onion and fry until softened, without allowing it to brown. Add the reserved tomato pulp, the rice and tomato purée. Season well with salt and pepper.

Bring the mixture to the boil and continue to cook for 10 minutes, stirring often. Stir in the parsley, dill, mint and lemon zest.

Fill the tomato shells with the rice mixture and top with their caps. Drizzle with the remaining oil, cover with foil and bake in the preheated oven for 1 hour until the rice is tender.

Serve warm from the oven or at room temperature.

Tomato basil salsa

Summer is the time for this classic bruschetta topping. Only make this one when you can get really great fresh tomatoes though, otherwise skip it.

450 g/1 lb. tomatoes (whichever kind you have to hand), halved and most of the seeds cut out, then finely diced
20 g/¾ oz. fresh basil leaves, finely chopped
1 garlic clove, grated
2 tablespoons good olive oil
1 teaspoon sherry vinegar
sea salt

MAKES 1 MEDIUM JAR

Combine all the ingredients together in a medium mixing bowl. Leave to stand for 15 minutes to let the flavours mingle. Taste and adjust the seasoning as desired.

Spiced red tomato chutney

This nicely spicy, rich chutney with a touch of heat is great with hamburgers.

3 cardamom pods, lightly crushed
3 whole cloves
1 cinnamon stick
1 kg/2¼ lb. ripe tomatoes, chopped, juices reserved
700 g/1½ lb. cooking apples, cored and finely chopped
300 g/10½ oz. onions, finely chopped
2 garlic cloves, chopped
2.5-cm/1-inch piece of fresh ginger, peeled and finely chopped
1 red chilli/chile, finely chopped
200 g/1⅓ cups sultanas/golden raisins
200 g/1 cup soft brown sugar
300 ml/1¼ cups white wine vinegar
2 teaspoons salt

sterilized glass jars

MAKES ABOUT 1.7 KG/3 PINTS

Wrap the cardamom pods, cloves and cinnamon stick in a small piece of muslin/cheesecloth to form a spice bag. Put the spice bag and all the other remaining ingredients in a large, non-reactive pan set over a medium heat.

Cook, stirring, until the sugar has dissolved. Cover and bring to the boil, then uncover and simmer for 2–3 hours, stirring now and then, until the mixture has reduced and thickened, with little excess moisture. Test the consistency by passing a wooden spoon through the mixture; if it leaves a clean channel as it passes, the chutney is ready.

Remove the spice bag and bottle at once in warm, sterilized jars (see page 4). Keep in a cool, dry place for 4–10 weeks to mature before eating. Once opened, store in the fridge.

Green tomato chutney

Unripe 'green' tomatoes, with their firm texture and slightly sour flavour, make an excellent tangy chutney.

1 cinnamon stick
4 whole cloves
4 allspice berries
5 black peppercorns
1 kg/2¼ lb. green tomatoes, chopped
750 g/1 lb. 10 oz. cooking apples, peeled, cored and finely chopped
300 g/10 oz. onions, chopped
150 g/1 cup sultanas/golden raisins
300 g/1½ cups light brown sugar
2 teaspoons salt
350 ml/1½ cups white wine vinegar
½ teaspoon Turkish/Aleppo pepper flakes

sterilized glass jars

MAKES ABOUT 1.4 KG/2½ PINTS

Place the cinnamon stick, cloves, allspice and peppercorns in a small muslin/cheesecloth bag. Put the spice bag and all the other remaining ingredients in a large, non-reactive pan set over a medium heat.

Bring the mixture to the boil and cook uncovered, stirring now and then, for 3 hours until it has thickened and reduced, but still has a little excess moisture.

Bottle and store following the instructions above.

KILNER

Blistered tomatoes

Roasting the tomatoes until just broken really intensifies the taste.

340 g/2 cups cherry or grape tomatoes, sliced in half
6–8 garlic cloves, crushed with the side of a wide knife
2 tablespoons olive oil
sea salt
bread, to serve

baking sheet, lined with baking parchment

SERVES 4–6

Preheat the oven to 200°C/180°C fan/400°F/gas 6. Scatter the tomatoes and garlic out on the prepared baking sheet. Drizzle with olive oil, season with salt and toss to combine. Roast in the preheated oven for 20–25 minutes until the tomatoes have collapsed and are beginning to turn golden. Serve with bread for mopping up the juices.

Heritage tomato fennel salad

Good, fresh tomatoes need little else to showcase them. Choose the best, varied tomatoes you can find and enjoy them, simply.

15 g/2 tablespoons flaked/slivered almonds
1 large fennel bulb
6–8 heritage tomatoes, ideally in assorted varieties
3 tablespoons extra virgin olive oil
1 tablespoon lemon juice
1 teaspoon sweet smoked paprika/pimentón
sea salt and black pepper

SERVES 4

Toast the flaked almonds in a small, dry heavy-bottomed frying pan/skillet until golden-brown. Swirl the pan regularly so that they don't burn. Remove from the pan and set aside.

Trim the fennel bulb, reserving the fronds, and slice very thinly. Cut the tomatoes into thin slices.

Mix together the oil, lemon juice and smoked paprika to make a dressing, seasoning with salt and pepper.

Arrange the fennel and tomato slices on a serving plate. Lightly toss with the dressing, sprinkle over the toasted almonds, garnish with the reserved fennel fronds and serve at once.

Cucumber & herb grain salad with lemon & mint labneh balls & grape dressing

Earthy grains, creamy labneh balls, fresh herbs, a red grape dressing and cucumber – all the best Mediterranean flavours that come together beautifully.

175 g/6 oz. bulgur wheat
1 vegetable stock/bouillon cube
1 teaspoon dried oregano
1 romaine lettuce heart, roughly chopped
2 Lebanese cucumbers, shaved into ribbons
25 g/1 oz. fresh mint leaves, chopped, plus extra to serve
6 spring onions/scallions, thinly sliced
30 g/1 oz. pistachios, chopped
Lemon & Mint Labneh balls (see below)

RED GRAPE DRESSING
3 tablespoons extra virgin olive oil
200 g/7 oz. red grapes, thinly sliced
3 tablespoons runny honey
2 tablespoons red wine vinegar
sea salt and black pepper

SERVES 4

Place the bulgur wheat, stock cube and dried oregano in a large bowl and cover with plenty of boiling hot water. Stir to mix together and dissolve the stock cube. Soak for 10–20 minutes until just tender but still a little al dente. Drain well, then tip onto a clean tea/dish towel and leave for 15 minutes or so to remove as much excess water as you can.

Make the dressing. Heat 1 tablespoon of the olive oil in a frying pan/skillet over a medium heat. Add the grapes and some seasoning and cook for 3 minutes. Add the remaining dressing ingredients and bring to the boil. Remove from the heat and set aside.

Tip the bulgur wheat into a mixing bowl. Stir in the lettuce, cucumber, mint, spring onions and grape dressing. Spoon onto a large serving platter and break over the minted labneh balls. Scatter over the pistachios and garnish with mint leaves. Serve straightaway while the lettuce is crunchy.

Lemon & mint labneh balls

150 g/5¼ oz. labneh
1 garlic clove, crushed
grated zest of 1 lemon
20 g/¾ oz. fresh mint leaves, finely chopped

Place the labneh in a bowl with the garlic and lemon zest. Stir together until combined and then roll the flavoured labneh into balls. Place the chopped mint on a plate, then roll the labneh balls in the mint to coat.

FLAVOUR VARIATIONS

Seed & spice Grind 1 teaspoon each coriander seeds and cumin seeds to a powder in a pestle and mortar. Mix with ½ teaspoon ground cinnamon, 1 teaspoon sesame seeds and a pinch of chilli/hot red pepper flakes. Roll plain labneh balls into the spice mix.

Pistachio & green olive Mix 100 g/3½ oz. finely chopped pistachios and 50 g/1¾ oz. finely chopped green olives, then roll plain labneh balls in the mixture.

Marinated Mix 7 tablespoons extra virgin olive oil with a halved red chilli, 1 sliced lemon and 3 sprigs of fresh rosemary. Place the rolled balls into the oil mixture. Keep refrigerated for up to a week.

Pimm's salad

Pimm's No. 1 Cup is traditionally served with mint, cucumber and a medley of chopped fresh summer fruits. This is my take, using the cocktail garnishes as a base for a quick and fun summery salad, perfect for al fresco lunches.

150 g/1½ cups strawberries, hulled and thinly sliced
1 large cucumber, peeled
small bunch of fresh mint
grated zest and juice of 1 lemon, plus lemon wedges to serve
50 g/1 cup fresh rocket/arugula
50 g/1 cup fresh watercress
150 ml/⅔ cup olive oil
20 ml/1½ tablespoons white wine vinegar
50 ml/3½ tablespoons Pimm's No. 1 cup or other summer gin cup

SERVES 4

Put the strawberries in a large mixing bowl and set aside.

Using a peeler, make long ribbons of the cucumber and add to the bowl with the strawberries. Discard the centre of the cucumber.

Pick two-thirds of the mint leaves and crush them a little before adding to the bowl; save the remaining leaves to dress the salad.

Add the lemon zest, rocket and watercress; checking they are cleaned and any large stalks are removed. Toss the leaves together to combine and coat in flavour.

Make a vinaigrette by pouring the lemon juice, olive oil, white wine vinegar and Pimm's into a jar with a screw-top lid. Tighten the lid and shake well to combine.

Pour about one-quarter of the vinaigrette down the side of the bowl with the salad ingredients and turn the salad over several times to coat.

To serve, arrange the salad on four plates and dress with the remaining mint leaves and a wedge of lemon. Pour the remaining vinaigrette into a jug/pitcher and bring to the table with a serving spoon.

Cucumber pickles

These crunchy pickles really pack a flavour punch. Add to any cheese board or snack plate.

2 cucumbers
1 tablespoon salt
120 g/4 oz. hijiki or arame seaweed
235 ml/scant 1 cup rice wine vinegar
180 g/scant 1 cup granulated sugar
1 teaspoon black sesame seeds

SERVES 6

Slice the cucumbers on the diagonal and spread out on a ceramic platter. Mix the salt into the cucumbers. Let stand for 10 minutes, then rinse and pat dry.

Place the seaweed in a small bowl and hydrate in a little warm water for 10 minutes, then drain and squeeze out the excess water.

Combine the vinegar and sugar in a medium saucepan with 235 ml/scant 1 cup water and bring to the boil. Take off the heat and add the cucumbers, seaweed and sesame seeds. Place in a sealable container, making sure the liquid is covering the cucumber, cool down, then refrigerate.

Try to let the flavours mellow for a few days before eating. Consume within 1 month.

Corn & quinoa fritters with crispy bacon & beetroot yogurt

Delicious little rosti-style fritters can be rustled up with almost any leftover vegetables that you have – sweetcorn/corn, courgettes/zucchini and carrots have been used here, with added crispy quinoa flakes. These are best served straight from the pan while still hot, and can be enjoyed with crispy bacon (but this is optional) and a garlicky yogurt and beet dip.

2 courgettes/zucchini, grated (about 250 g/9 oz.)
2 carrots, grated (about 200 g/7 oz.)
2 corn cobs, kernels removed (about 200 g/7 oz.)
½ bunch of coriander/cilantro, finely chopped
1 bunch of spring onions/scallions, finely chopped
1 teaspoon ground coriander
1 green chilli/chile, finely chopped
100 g/1 cup chickpea/garbanzo bean (gram) flour
190 g/2 cups quinoa flakes
4 eggs, lightly beaten
180 g/6½ oz. streaky/fatty bacon
3 tablespoons olive oil
sea salt and black pepper

BEETROOT/BEET YOGURT
200 g/scant 1 cup Greek yogurt
1 garlic clove, crushed
1 raw beetroot/beet, peeled and grated
1 teaspoon ground coriander
juice of 1 lime
1 tablespoon olive oil

TO SERVE
fresh coriander/cilantro leaves
lime wedges

SERVES 4–6

Start by removing the excess moisture from the grated courgettes by wrapping them in muslin/cheesecloth and squeezing out excess moisture. Combine the courgettes, carrots, corn, coriander, spring onions, ground coriander and green chilli in a bowl.

Place chickpea flour, quinoa, eggs and 150 ml/⅔ cup water in a bowl. Whisk to combine. Season with salt and pepper. Pour the batter into the bowl of vegetables and mix well to combine, then set aside for 30 minutes.

Meanwhile, preheat the oven to 180°C/160°C fan/350°F/gas 4. Lay the bacon slices in a single layer on a baking sheet (do not let them overlap or they will stick together). Bake for about 20 minutes, depending on its thickness, until the bacon is crispy. Keep warm.

Make the beetroot yogurt by mixing all the ingredients in a bowl, season well and taste.

Heat the olive oil in a frying pan/skillet over a medium heat. Add 1 heaped tablespoon/¼ cup measures of fritter mixture to the pan. Cook for 4 minutes on each side and drain on paper towels. Repeat with the remaining mixture and keep warm.

Serve the fritters with the bacon and beetroot yogurt and topped with coriander leaves and lime wedges. Chilli jam and chopped spring onions also go well.

Corn cobs with salted chilli olive oil

Everyone assumes that only butter makes the best buttery taste, but it is simply not true. A good-quality virgin olive oil is the perfect addition to whip up the creamiest mash, or for smothering some plump, seasonal vegetables. It is really easy to find good-quality olive oil these days and the flavour profiles can be sublime. You'll be surprised how much you don't miss the butter.

140 ml/scant ⅔ cup good-quality olive oil
½ tablespoon Himalayan rock salt
1–2 teaspoons dried chilli flakes/ hot red pepper flakes
4 corn cobs, trimmed and halved

SERVES 4

In a large bowl, mix together the olive oil, salt and chilli flakes and set aside for 20–30 minutes.

Preheat the oven to 220°C/200° fan/425°F/gas 7.

Place a corn cob on a large foil square, spoon over some of the chilli oil mix and then wrap well in the foil. Repeat for each of the cobs and reserve the bowl with the remaining oil. Place the cobs on a baking sheet in the preheated oven and roast for 45–50 minutes until the corn is cooked.

Remove the cobs from the foil and tip them back into the large bowl with the remaining spicy oil. Toss them around so that they are well coated, then serve immediately.

Roast vegetable cassoulet with sizzled artichokes

This version of the French cassoulet is based on vegetables, rather than the usual array of pork and duck, with the artichokes adding taste and texture. Vegetables cook at an uneven rate, so if you are doing them all together, as here, you can make life a bit easier by cutting the ones that take longer to cook – notably carrots – into smaller pieces than those that soften more quickly – for instance, squash.

- 2 tablespoons olive oil, plus a little extra to drizzle
- 2–3 artichokes (either chargrilled from a jar, or canned) drained and dried well
- 500 g/1 lb. 2 oz. total weight of any combination of these vegetables: carrots, celery, butternut squash, courgettes/zucchini, celeriac/celery root, or parsnips, sliced or chopped into bite-size chunks
- 230-g/8-oz. can chopped tomatoes, or ½ a 400-g/14-oz. can
- 100 ml/⅓ cup red or white wine or water
- 400-g/14-oz. can haricot /navy beans, drained and rinsed
- 2 teaspoons Dijon or wholegrain mustard
- 1 tablespoon chopped fresh flat-leaf parsley
- 2–3 handfuls of panko crumbs
- sea salt and black pepper

SERVES 2

Preheat the oven to 200°C/180°C fan/400°F/gas 6.

Heat half the oil in a large ovenproof frying pan/skillet. Slice the artichokes into slivers, add them to the pan and sizzle over a medium-high heat until golden on all sides – 3–5 minutes. Set aside on a small plate.

Add the remaining 1 tablespoon of oil, the prepared vegetables and plenty of seasoning to the pan. Toss well over a high heat, then transfer to the oven and roast for about 30 minutes until tender. Check each vegetable in turn and continue roasting until tender if necessary. Turn the oven up to 220°C/200°C fan/425°F/gas 7.

Stir in the tomatoes, wine, drained beans, mustard and parsley. Bring to the boil on the hob/stovetop, then sprinkle on the panko crumbs so you have a thin layer over the entire surface, add the reserved artichokes, drizzle with a little oil and bake for 5–10 minutes until the top is lightly browned. Leave to cool for 10 minutes before serving.

TIP

- *To serve to non-vegetarians, this dish also works well when accompanied by a sausage or two.*

Artichokes with garlic butter

Stunning to look at and simple to cook, an artichoke often scares cooks due to its rugged appearance and often complicated methods to cook and prepare. Artichokes are at their best when simply cooked and served with garlic butter as finger food. Serve with plenty of napkins and a teaspoon to remove the choke.

4 globe artichokes
200 g/1¾ sticks butter
2 garlic cloves, crushed
50 g/½ cup grated Parmesan cheese
black pepper

SERVES 4

Trim the base of each artichoke so it can stand upright. Slice across the artichoke top, about 3 cm/1¼ inch from the top, to display the inner leaf patterns.

Transfer the artichokes to a large covered pan of salted water and simmer over a low heat for 30 minutes.

Heat the butter in a small pan until it just begins to foam. Add the crushed garlic to the foaming butter and remove from the heat; stir a couple of times to distribute the garlic and set aside.

Place the steaming hot artichokes in four serving bowls. Drizzle with the garlic butter and top with Parmesan. Finish with a sprinkle of black pepper and serve.

To eat the artichoke, pluck each petal and squeeze the petal between your teeth pulling out the fleshy centre from the base. When all the petals have been eaten, remove the furry choke with a teaspoon then eat the core of the artichoke, mopping up the remaining butter and cheese. This is messy eating at its delicious best!

TIP

- *When selecting your artichokes in the supermarket/grocery store, give them a squeeze; if they squeak then they're ripe and a good choice. Look for ones that feel heavy and solid and are about 7.5–12 cm/3–5 inches in diameter and make sure the leaves are tightly packed.*

Pods & Beans

PEAS | MANGETOUT | BROAD BEANS | GREEN BEANS

Gnocchi with peas, mascarpone & black garlic

Traditionally, potato gnocchi dumplings are boiled, but frying them instead adds interest to the texture and a little extra flavour. It also saves on washing up, as you can make the whole dish in one pan, which is always a win.

1 black garlic clove, peeled
30 g/2 tablespoons butter
1 tablespoon olive oil
250 g/9 oz. store-bought potato gnocchi
125 g/1 cup mascarpone
120 g/1 cup frozen peas (no need to defrost)
good pinch of crushed chillies/ hot red pepper flakes
100 g/3½ oz. baby spinach leaves
3 tablespoons freshly grated Parmesan, plus extra to serve
2 tablespoons toasted pine nuts

SERVES 2

Mash together the black garlic and butter and set aside.

Heat the oil in a small frying pan/skillet and fry the gnocchi for about 5 minutes until golden. Lower the heat and add the mascarpone to melt, along with the peas and crushed chillies. Bring to a gentle simmer, then stir in the spinach leaves, just until wilted.

When hot through and the spinach has wilted, stir in the black garlic butter and grated Parmesan, and serve sprinkled with the toasted pine nuts and extra grated Parmesan, if you wish.

Pea & wasabi dip

A quick recipe that makes use of the freezer and store cupboard to whip up a fresh and spicy dip for afternoon snacking. The punchy flavour and heat of wasabi is quite addictive!

½ small red onion, finely diced
white wine vinegar, to cover
150 g/1¼ cup frozen peas, slightly defrosted
1 teaspoon wasabi powder
1 teaspoon light soy sauce
grated zest of 1 lemon
sea salt
crudités or crackers, to serve

SERVES 4

Put the onion in a small bowl and just cover with the vinegar. Set aside to infuse for 15 minutes.

Put the peas, wasabi, soy sauce and lemon zest in a jug/pitcher. Use a handheld stick blender to purée the contents to make a smooth, thick paste. Taste and, if you like your dip hotter, add a little more wasabi, then blend again.

Add a heaped teaspoon of drained red onion pieces and a good pinch of salt. Mix together with a spoon. Serve as a dip with crudités or on crackers.

Pea & olive pistou

This fresh-tasting, flavourful pistou has a multitude of uses. Serve as a dip with crudités, drizzled on top of soup, or with grilled meats and fish.

1 garlic clove, crushed
150 ml/⅔ cup olive oil
150 g/1¼ cups fresh or frozen peas, blanched
50 g/1¾ oz. Nocellara olives, pitted and chopped
3 sprigs fresh mint, leaves picked
1 sprig fresh tarragon, leaves picked
juice of ½ lemon
sea salt

MAKES 1 SMALL JAR

Pulse the garlic, a pinch of sea salt and 100 ml/⅓ cup of the olive oil in a food processor. Add the peas, olives, mint, tarragon and lemon juice. Check the consistency (it should be similar to pesto) and add the extra oil if needed. Adjust the seasoning and use as required.

The pistou will keep in the fridge for 2 days.

Farro risotto with green peas

Farro risotto uses this sturdy grain in the place of short-grain rice and adds a pleasant nuttiness and texture to a risotto.

1 teaspoon chopped dried porcini or shiitake mushrooms
950 ml/4 cups vegetable stock
2 tablespoons olive oil or butter
2 leeks, thinly sliced into half-moons
4 garlic cloves, finely chopped
185 g/1 cup farro

PEA PURÉE
125 g/1 cup frozen peas
2 big handfuls of fresh spinach
1 tablespoon lemon juice
sea salt

TO GARNISH
grated Parmesan (optional)
toasted pine nuts
fresh basil, finely chopped

SERVES 4

In a medium saucepan, combine the dried mushrooms and vegetable stock and bring to a gentle simmer.

Meanwhile, in a large saucepan with high sides, heat the olive oil or butter over a medium-high heat. Add the leeks and garlic and cook, stirring, for about 6–8 minutes until the leeks are softened, adding a little splash of water if the mixture becomes too dry.

Add the farro and stir to coat in the olive oil and leeks and toast for about 2 minutes. Add the stock one ladleful at a time, every 3–4 minutes, stirring once or twice and then letting it bubble until the liquid evaporates. Repeat until all the stock has been added and the farro is tender and creamy, about 40 minutes.

Meanwhile, thaw the frozen peas in a medium bowl by pouring boiling water over to submerge and covering with a lid. Let stand for 5 minutes. Drain and transfer the peas to a blender or food processor. Add the spinach, a pinch or two of salt and the lemon juice. Purée until smooth-ish.

Finish the farro risotto by stirring in some Parmesan (if using) and dividing among serving bowls. Top each bowl with the pea purée and swirl it in to mix. Top with toasted pine nuts, basil and more Parmesan, if desired.

Pea & mint soup

Pea and mint is the freshest combination and when combined in this delicious soup, makes the perfect light-tasting springtime soup.

60 g/4 tablespoons butter
2 leeks, trimmed and chopped
200 g/7 oz. potatoes, chopped
1 garlic clove, crushed
750 g/6 cups frozen peas
1 litre/4 cups chicken or veg stock
2 fresh mint sprigs
sea salt and black pepper

SERVES 6

Melt the butter in a saucepan, add the leeks, potatoes and garlic and fry for 10 minutes. Add the peas, stock, mint and a little salt and pepper and bring to the boil. Cover and simmer for 20 minutes. Discard the mint sprigs.

Transfer the soup to a food processor or blender and purée until smooth. Return to the pan, season to taste and heat through before serving.

Eggy bread with peas & capers

A childhood favourite of eggy bread with ketchup here gets a makeover with this more grown-up savoury version, and the addition of peas mean you still get a natural sweetness in the finished dish. This works with whatever bread you have to hand, either fresh or straight from the freezer.

2 eggs
30 ml/2 tablespoons whole milk
30 g/2 tablespoons unsalted butter
4 slices of bread
20 g/2 tablespoons capers, drained
100 g/¾ cup frozen peas
sea salt and black pepper

SERVES 2

Preheat the oven to 120°C/100°C fan/250°F/gas ½. Place an ovenproof plate on the bottom shelf of the oven.

Whisk the eggs and milk in a shallow bowl with a generous pinch of seasoning. Heat half the butter in a non-stick frying pan/skillet over a medium heat.

Add a slice of bread to the egg bowl and slosh it around so it absorbs some of the egg mixture, then flip it over and slosh around once more.

Once the butter has melted and is gently sizzling in the pan, transfer the eggy bread to the pan and fry for about 3 minutes on each side, until both sides are golden brown and crispy-edged. While the first slice is cooking, place a second piece of bread in the egg bowl to soak.

When the first slice of bread is done, transfer it to the warming plate in the oven and cook the next slice in the same way. Repeat the process until all 4 slices have been cooked. Use the remaining butter as needed.

When the pan is empty, pop the capers and peas straight in, with a small splash of water and twist of pepper. Fry for about 3 minutes until they're tender and starting to catch a little. As they cook, gently mash them in the pan with the back of a fork. Taste to check for seasoning.

Halve the eggy bread, divide between serving plates, then pile the peas and capers on top and serve immediately.

TIP

- *Chop the bread up a bit and fry it all together in a large pan. Serve with fresh tomatoes and salad, like crunchy, eggy croutons and greens.*

Greens on toast

This recipe can use whatever greens you have, whether they be fresh or frozen, sturdy or limping. Just get them in a pan with some lemon and chilli/chile and you're good to go. It's also great with an egg on top, if you so wish. Very, very simple, super quick and a delicious lunch when working at home. Best eaten with the sun on your face if possible.

200 g/7 oz. greens (mangetout/ snow peas, spinach, broccoli, cabbage, pak choi/bok choi, edamame, peas, broad/fava beans, green/French beans, sugar snaps, kale, cavolo nero, chard, beetroot/ beet leaves, radish tops, rocket/ arugula, endive, watercress, spring greens...)
a knob/pat of butter
2 large slices of bread
pinch (or two) of dried chilli/ hot red pepper flakes
squeeze of lemon juice
extra virgin olive oil, to serve

SERVES 2

Roughly slice the greens if they need it, but leave delicate/smaller leaves whole (spinach, rocket, beetroot tops). Add the butter to a large frying pan/skillet set over a medium heat. Pop the bread in the toaster (or under the grill/broiler).

Once the butter is sizzling, add the greens with a good pinch of seasoning and chilli flakes and fry for 3–5 minutes until wilted and fairly tender, but still vibrant, green and with a bite. Add a good squeeze of lemon juice and remove from the heat.

Put the toast on a serving plate and pile on the buttery, lemony greens, drizzling any pan butter over. Finish with a drizzle of olive oil and an extra pinch of chilli flakes if you like. Serve immediately.

TIP

- *If your greens are light and leafy, they'll only take a minute or two in the pan, so if using a mixture, add the thicker or hardier ones first (broccoli, beans, thick cabbage, mange tout etc) and give them 3–5 minutes in the pan, then add the leafy greens (spinach, kale, cavolo nero, rocket, peas etc) for a minute or two at the end, just to wilt and tenderize.*

Braised broad beans & peas with mint & trofie pasta

A light summer bowl of pasta, gently braised with broad/fava beans and peas for a gentle, flavour. This is easily made vegan by omitting the pancetta and using vegan cheese.

250 g/9 oz. broad/fava beans (podded weight)
150 g/1¼ cup frozen garden peas
300 g/10½ oz. trofie pasta
2 tablespoons olive oil
8 thin pancetta slices (optional)
2 garlic cloves, crushed
50 ml/3½ tablespoons white wine
100 ml/⅓ cup vegetable stock
3 tablespoons fresh mint leaves, chopped, plus extra to garnish
4 tablespoons grated Parmesan (or a vegan option)
black pepper

SERVES 4

Cook the broad beans and peas in a large saucepan of boiling salted water for 2–3 minutes until tender. Scoop them into a sieve with a slotted spoon (reserving the water), then refresh under cold water. Bring the water back to the boil and cook the pasta according to the pack instructions.

Meanwhile, remove and discard the outer skin from the broad beans, and set aside with the peas.

Heat the olive oil in a frying pan/skillet over a medium heat and cook the pancetta slices, if using, for 4–6 minutes until golden and crispy. Transfer to a plate lined with paper towels.

In the same pan, add the garlic and white wine and cook down for a few minutes, then add the vegetable stock and cook for a few more minutes. Add the podded broad beans and peas and cook gently for 1 minute.

Drain the pasta and return to the saucepan. Tip in the bean mixture and add the mint and half the Parmesan, tossing together. Break up the pancetta, if using, and toss into the pasta. Serve in bowls with the remaining Parmesan, some black pepper and some mint leaves to garnish.

Broad bean hummus

The nutty flavour of broad/fava beans works well with lemon and the sesame of the tahini.

300 g/2¼ cups broad/fava beans (podded weight)
400-g/14-oz can chickpeas/garbanzo beans, drained and rinsed
50 g/¼ cup tahini
2 cloves of roasted confit garlic (usually sold in jars) (optional)
grated zest and juice of 1 lemon
sea salt and black pepper

SERVES 4

Put the broad beans in a pan of cold, unsalted water and set over a medium heat. Bring to a low simmer and cook for 5 minutes. Drain, then put in a bowl of cold water and chill in the fridge to halt the cooking. After a few minutes, remove the outer skins and discard, reserving the inner beans.

Put the beans and the remaining ingredients in a large mixing bowl with a pinch of salt. Blend to a paste using a handheld stick blender. Taste the mixture and add extra salt if needed. Sprinkle with black pepper and serve with toasted bread or cover and store in the fridge for up to 4 days.

Green vegetable medley

Follow this method, swapping the selection of greens to suit what is in season, what you have to hand or whatever you fancy.

1 garlic clove, sliced
2 tablespoons olive oil
1 small head of broccoli, broken into florets
½ sweetheart cabbage, shredded
180 g/6½ oz. green/French beans, trimmed, or prepared runner beans
150 ml/⅔ cup chicken or vegetable stock, white wine or water
125 g/1 cup frozen or fresh peas or petits pois
30 g/2 tablespoons butter
sea salt and black pepper

SERVES 4

Fry the garlic for a few seconds in the oil in a frying pan/skillet. Add the broccoli, cabbage and beans and stir fry for 5 minutes. Pour in the liquid and add the peas. Keeping it on a high heat, cover immediately and leave to steam for 3–4 minutes. Remove the lid, letting the steam escape and continue on the heat until just a little liquid is left.

Remove from the heat, stir in the butter and season with salt and pepper before serving.

Tray-baked greens

Try this simple one-pan recipe for green vegetables roasted with a splash of rosé and butter and you won't be disappointed! Perfect served with simply cooked chicken breast or fish.

100 g/3½ oz. fine green/French beans, trimmed
2 garlic cloves, sliced
125 ml/½ cup dry rosé or white wine
85 g/¾ stick butter, cubed
splash of olive oil
500 g/1 lb. 2 oz. fresh asparagus spears, woody ends trimmed
100 g/⅔ cup frozen or fresh petits pois or peas
1 fresh tarragon sprig, leaves picked
large handful of baby leaf spinach or other robust green salad leaves
juice of 1 lemon
sea salt and black pepper

SERVES 4 AS A SIDE

Preheat the oven to 220°C/200°C fan/425°F/gas 7.

Place the green beans, garlic, wine, butter and a splash of olive oil in a deep-sided roasting pan. Toss to mix everything together and season generously with salt and pepper. Bake, uncovered, in the preheated oven for 8 minutes, then remove from the oven but don't turn the oven off.

Fold in the asparagus spears, petits pois and tarragon, giving the pan a good shake to help combine the wine and butter. Return the pan to the oven to cook for a further 8 minutes.

Remove from the oven and immediately fold in the baby spinach, ensuring everything is coated in the buttery juices. Squeeze the lemon over the whole lot and gently mix it all together.

Transfer to a shallow serving dish, discarding any leftover liquid, and then serve immediately.

Leaves, Greens & Brassicas

SALAD LEAVES | SPINACH | CHARD | KALE | BRUSSELS SPROUTS | CABBAGE | BROCCOLI | CAULIFLOWER

Chicken salad with orange, avocado & dates

You won't find an easier or lovelier summer lunch or supper than this. You can make it with leftover roast chicken, but it is also excellent with bought, cooked chicken pieces, which also have the advantage that you can ring the flavour changes. Cajun chicken works well, because the gentle spiciness gives a coronation chicken feel to the dish.

1 orange
175 g/6 oz. cooked chicken pieces, such as Cajun or flame-grilled, sliced into bite-size pieces
1 endive/chicory bulb, halved crossways and slivered
1 ripe avocado, peeled, stoned/pitted and sliced or cubed
3 Medjool dates, stoned/pitted, each sliced into 6 pieces
4 tablespoons mayonnaise
1 teaspoon any chopped fresh or frozen herbs
2 tablespoons flaked/slivered almonds, toasted

SERVES 2

Segment the orange by slicing off the peel, then cut out the individual segments and put in a medium bowl. If you have juice on the board, tip it into a second bowl, squeezing any juice you can from the orange peel and discarded membrane, so you have about 1 tablespoon. (If this seems like a faff, simply remove the peel and slice it into rounds instead.)

Add the chicken, endive, avocado and dates to the bowl with the orange segments. Season generously.

Add the mayonnaise and herbs to the orange juice and mix. Pour over the salad and toss to mix. Top with the nuts just before serving.

TIP

- *Endive/chicory is inexpensive and readily available, but you are often corralled into buying a bag of four or six bulbs, when one would suffice. The separated leaves are delicious used as a dipper for hummus or any other fresh tasting dip if you need to use any leftover endive up.*

Caesar salad 'green goddess'

This dish is a riff on Caesar salad with an avocado and herb dressing. The lettuce here is important, and it's worth seeking out small Cos/Romaine or Little Gem. You can turn this into something more substantial by adding slivers of cooked chicken (such as chargrilled) or flakes of smoked mackerel in step 3.

1 small Cos/Romaine or 2 Little Gem lettuces, broken into bite-size pieces
4 anchovy fillets, cut into very thin slivers (see right for other options)
2 tablespoons freshly grated Parmesan, plus extra to serve
sea salt and black pepper

CROÛTONS
1 tablespoon butter
1 garlic clove, halved down the centre
1 slice of white bread, crusts removed, cut into large dice

DRESSING
3 tablespoons mayonnaise
3 tablespoons soured cream
½ ripe avocado, peeled and stoned
large bunch of fresh herbs, ideally tarragon and parsley, roughly chopped
juice of ½ lemon

SERVES 2

Melt the butter in a medium frying pan/skillet and fry the garlic, bread and seasoning gently for 8–10 minutes until golden, turning and shaking constantly. When done, pick out and discard the garlic but leave the croûtons in the pan.

Crush the softened garlic into the bowl of a small food processor and add the other dressing ingredients plus plenty of seasoning. Whizz until smooth. Add a splash of water if it is too thick to drizzle.

Put the remaining salad ingredients in a bowl and toss with most of the dressing. Put on plates, scatter the croûtons artfully on top and drizzle with the remaining dressing. Sprinkle over some extra Parmesan to serve.

TIP

- *Anchovies have a unique flavour, but not everyone cares for it. For meat-eaters, crisply fried bacon strips make an appealing alternative here. If you are not eating meat, olives or capers work well.*

Spanakopita strudel

Filo/phyllo pastry is wonderful stuff, but it comes in a perplexing range of sizes – whatever size you start off with, simply follow step 2 and you will be good to go. If you wish, you can make a simple (optional) Greek salad as you go along. A potential further embellishment is tzatziki, made by mixing Greek yogurt, grated cucumber, crushed garlic and chopped herbs with plenty of seasoning; you can loosen the consistency with a splash of water, if you wish.

250 g/9 oz. fresh or frozen spinach leaves, cooked (or defrosted), chopped and squeezed to give 150–175 g/¾–1 cup of prepared spinach
50 g/1¾ oz. feta, crumbled
50 g/¼ cup ricotta
3 spring onions/scallions, chopped
1 tablespoon toasted pine nuts
1 tablespoon chopped fresh or frozen herbs, such as parsley, chives, dill and mint
juice of ½ lemon
1 garlic clove, crushed
freshly grated nutmeg
2 tablespoons grated Parmesan
135 g/4¾ oz. filo/phyllo pastry
2 tablespoons butter, melted
sprinkling of nigella seeds, to finish (optional)
sea salt and black pepper

GREEK SALAD
50 g/1¾ oz. feta, sliced or cubed
1 spring onion/scallion, chopped
1 tablespoon chopped fresh herbs
squeeze of lemon juice
1–2 tomatoes, deseeded and diced
¼ cucumber, diced
12 Kalamata olives, stoned/pitted
olive oil or vinaigrette, to serve

SERVES 2

Mix the first 10 ingredients thoroughly in a bowl with plenty of seasoning – check to taste, as it needs to be boldly flavoured.

Layer up sheets of filo on a piece of baking parchment to form a rough 25-cm/10-inch square about 8 sheets thick, cutting or folding and buttering as you go. Arrange the filling evenly along the bottom edge of the pastry and use the baking parchment to help you roll it up to form a log (leave the ends open). Transfer, on the paper, to a baking sheet. Use your sharpest knife to make 4 slashes in the top of the pastry (right through to the filling). Brush with the remains of the melted butter and sprinkle with nigella seeds, if using.

Bake at 200°C/180°C fan/400°F/gas 6 for about 25 minutes until golden all over. (No need to preheat your oven but it will save you 5 minutes if you do.) Remove from the oven and leave to cool for 10–15 minutes before slicing and serving with tzatziki (see intro), if you wish.

To make the Greek salad, simply mix the prepared ingredients and season generously. Set aside until ready to eat, dressing at the last minute.

Ham, spinach & mozzarella galettes

Once you have the knack of this generous supper dish, you can flavour it up it according to the season or your mood by using whatever ingredients you have to hand.

250 g/9 oz. fresh or frozen spinach, cooked (or defrosted), chopped and squeezed dry
100 g/3½ oz. cooked ham, cut into 2-cm/¾-inch cubes
125-g/4½-oz. mozzarella ball, drained and shredded
1 garlic clove, crushed
freshly grated nutmeg
finely grated zest of ½ lemon
3 tablespoons grated Parmesan
1 egg
300 g/10½ oz. ready-made puff pastry
2 tablespoons pine nuts
splash of milk
sea salt and black pepper

SERVES 2

Put the first 6 ingredients plus 2 tablespoons of the Parmesan in a mixing bowl. Beat the egg lightly, set aside 2 teaspoons in a small bowl for the glaze, then add the rest to the mixing bowl and mix. Check the seasoning, though it doesn't need much on account of the ham and cheese.

For the pastry, you need 2 circles of about 25 cm/10 inch in diameter, or equivalent ovals. Roll out as necessary and trim any corners. Spoon the filling into the centre of each circle, leaving a 3-cm/1¼-inch border round the edge. Now fold up the edges, crimping lightly as you go. You can refrigerate at this point for a couple of hours, if convenient.

When ready to bake, preheat the oven to 200°C/180°C fan/400°F/gas 6.

Sprinkle the exposed filling with the remaining Parmesan and the pine nuts. Add a splash of milk to the reserved egg and brush the mixture over the pastry to glaze. Bake for about 20 minutes until puffed and golden (the galettes will sink once they are removed from the oven).

Spinach & chickpea curry

This vibrantly-coloured, aromatic curry really showcases the freshness of spinach.

1 onion, roughly chopped
2 garlic cloves, sliced
1 teaspoon chopped fresh ginger
1 tablespoon light olive oil
2 tablespoons mild curry paste
400-g/14-oz. can chopped tomatoes
400-g/14-oz. can chickpeas/garbanzo beans, drained and rinsed
500 g/1 lb. 2 oz. spinach, chopped
handful of chopped fresh coriander/cilantro

SERVES 4

Put the onion, garlic and ginger in a food processor and process until finely chopped. Heat the oil in a frying pan/skillet set over a high heat. Add the onion mixture and cook for 4–5 minutes, stirring often, until golden. Add the curry paste and stir-fry for just 2 minutes until aromatic. Stir in the tomatoes, 250 ml/1 cup cold water and the chickpeas.

Bring to the boil, then reduce the heat to a medium simmer and cook, uncovered, for 10 minutes. Stir in the spinach and cook just until it is wilted. Stir in the coriander and serve with the Indian bread of your choice.

Spinach tomato soufflé

A light-textured soufflé, presented straight from the oven, makes an elegant meal. Serve this with a crisp green side salad.

500 g/1 lb. 2 oz. fresh spinach
300 g/10½ oz. ripe tomatoes
½ tablespoon olive oil
1 small onion, finely chopped
1 bay leaf
1 tablespoon tomato purée/paste
50 g/3 tablespoons butter
50 g/5 tablespoons flour
200 ml/¾ cup warm whole milk
5 eggs, separated, plus 1 egg white
sea salt and black pepper
freshly grated nutmeg

2 litre/1 quart soufflé dish, greased

SERVES 6

Preheat the oven to 200°C/180°C fan/400°F/gas 6.

Rinse the spinach under cold, running water. Put it in a saucepan or pot, cover with boiling water and set over a medium heat. Cook for 2–3 minutes until wilted; drain, cool, squeeze dry and roughly chop.

Next, scald the tomatoes. Pour boiling water over the ripe tomatoes in a heatproof bowl. Set aside for 1 minute, then drain and carefully peel off the skin using a sharp knife. Roughly chop, reserving any juices, and set aside.

Heat the oil in a frying pan/skillet set over a medium heat. Add the onion and bay leaf and fry for 2 minutes until softened. Add the chopped tomatoes and their juices, cover and cook for 5 minutes. Uncover, mix with a wooden spoon to help the tomatoes break down, stir in the tomato purée and cook, uncovered, for 5 minutes to form a thick sauce. Remove and discard the bay leaf.

In a separate heavy-bottomed saucepan or pot set over a medium heat, melt the butter. Mix in the flour, stirring well. Gradually stir in the warm milk and cook, stirring continuously, until it thickens. Season with salt, pepper and nutmeg.

Remove the white sauce from heat. Mix in the tomato sauce, then the spinach. Check and adjust the seasoning if necessary. Beat in the egg yolks, one at a time, and set aside.

Whisk the egg whites until stiff peaks form. Stir a spoonful of the whisked egg white into the soufflé mixture to loosen it. Lightly and gently fold in the remaining whisked egg white. Pour into the prepared soufflé dish and bake in the preheated oven for 1 hour until the soufflé is risen and golden brown. Serve at once.

Rainbow chard & Comté quiche

Chard and Comté quiche is a classic French dish, with this version using rainbow chard for added colour. If you can't find Comté, or struggle to find a vegetarian Comté-style cheese, it can be substituted with Gruyère cheese.

200 g/7 oz. all-butter shortcrust pastry
2 shallots, finely diced
large bunch of rainbow chard, roughly chopped
150 g/5¼ oz. Comté cheese, finely grated
6 eggs
200 ml/¾ cup double/heavy cream
200 ml/¾ cup whole milk
pinch of ground mace
sea salt and black pepper
butter, for frying
green salad, to serve (optional)

deep fluted 25-cm/10-inch tart pan, greased

SERVES 4

Preheat the oven to 180°C/160°C fan/350°F/gas 4.

Roll the pastry out on a lightly floured surface to a thickness of about 3 mm/⅛ inch. Gently drape it over a rolling pin and transfer to the tart pan, covering it and overlapping the sides. With the pastry in place, use a fork to prick the base repeatedly, about 5 mm/¼ inch apart, then set in the fridge for 15 minutes to firm up.

Blind bake in the preheated oven for 10 minutes to set the pastry and make the quiche base. Remove and trim off any excess pastry around the top to create a smooth edge. Leave the oven on but turn it down to 160°C/140°C fan/325°F/gas 3.

Put the shallots in a large frying pan/skillet with enough butter to cover the base when heated. Set over a high heat until the butter is sizzling, then add the chard, cooking and turning it for a few minutes, until it begins to wilt.

Transfer the chard and shallot mixture in a sieve/strainer and, using the back of a wooden spoon, squeeze out any excess liquid.

Cover the base of the quiche with the chard and shallot mixture, then sprinkle the Comté cheese over the top.

Whisk together the eggs, cream, milk, mace, salt and pepper. Pour into the quiche base until just below the rim.

Bake in the oven for 45–50 minutes until the mixture just starts to set in the middle. Remove from the oven and rest for 10 minutes to finish cooking. Serve hot or cold with a green salad if desired.

Avocado & kale grain bowl with tahini-coriander dressing

This salad can be prepared ahead for either a light lunch at home or for lunch boxes. Pouches of ready-cooked mixed grains, with extra flavours added, can be bought from most supermarkets.

- bunch of kale, stems discarded, torn into bite-sized pieces
- 3 tablespoons extra-virgin olive oil
- grated zest and juice of 2 lemons
- 4 spring onions/scallions, finely chopped
- 400-g/14-oz. can chickpeas/garbanzo beans, drained and rinsed
- 400 g/14 oz. mixed cooked grains
- 120 g/4 oz. feta, crumbled (or vegan equivalent)
- 1 avocado, halved, stoned/pitted and peeled
- 2 tablespoons dukkah, plus extra to finish
- 1 courgette/zucchini, grated
- 50 g/½ cup stoned/pitted green olives
- pistachio nuts, coarsely chopped, to serve

TAHINI-CORIANDER/CILANTRO DRESSING

- 30 g/1 oz. fresh coriander/cilantro, leaves and stalks
- 1 teaspoon ground coriander
- 1 teaspoon ground cumin
- 70 ml/scant ⅓ cup extra virgin olive oil
- 60 ml/¼ cup tahini
- 1 garlic clove, crushed
- juice of 1 lemon
- sea salt and black pepper

SERVES 2

Combine the kale, olive oil and lemon juice and zest in a bowl, season and massage kale with your fingers until it wilts. Add the spring onions, chickpeas and mixed grains, and toss to combine.

For the dressing, whisk the ingredients together in a bowl, then thin with 2–3 tablespoons of hot water to drizzling consistency and season to taste.

Divide the kale mixture between 2 serving bowls and scatter with the feta. Dip one half of the cut-side of the avocado in dukkah, place on top of the kale mixture and arrange the courgette and olives next to it. Drizzle with the dressing to taste and serve scattered with pistachio nuts.

Apple & kale salad

The sweetness of an apple and the super savouriness of kale and Parmesan are what make this salad marvellous. If it's not the right time of year for adding asparagus to the recipe, simply leave it out. You could replace it with something like green beans or use more broccoli.

100 g/3½ oz. Tenderstem broccoli (or standard broccoli)
100 g/3½ oz. asparagus (if in season)
100 g/3½ oz. kale
1 lemon
1 Braeburn apple
100 g/3½ oz. rocket/arugula
2 tablespoons extra virgin olive oil
25 g/¼ cup grated Parmesan
sea salt and black pepper
olive oil, for roasting

SERVES 4

Preheat the oven to 220°C/200°C fan/425°F/gas 7.

Halve the broccoli widthways, and trim the base of the asparagus. If you're using standard broccoli, then chop up, including the trunk, into small florets.

Add the broccoli and asparagus to a large baking sheet, drizzle with olive oil and season. Toss to coat and then bake on the top shelf of the oven for 8 minutes.

Add the kale to a large salad bowl and drizzle with a small amount of olive oil, season and then toss, crunching slightly with your hands to combine.

Core and quarter the apple and thinly slice each quarter lengthways. Halve the lemon and then squeeze some juice over the apple slices.

Once the vegetables have had 8 minutes, remove from the oven and tip the kale on top, then spread out. Return to the oven for another 10–12 minutes until the kale is crispy, but not burnt.

Add the apple slices, rocket, extra virgin olive oil, grated Parmesan and a good squeeze of lemon juice to the salad bowl and set aside.

Once the greens are ready, let them cool down on the baking sheet for 5 minutes, then add to the salad bowl and toss well to combine. Season to taste and serve.

TIP

- *This salad is delicious loaded up in a baguette with some very mature Cheddar cheese, some chutney and roasted ham, or just serve it up as it is with some extra salad leaves folded through.*

Cayenne-roasted sprouts with chickpeas & apricots

Although boiling is most people's go-to method, Brussels sprouts are also delicious when eaten raw, sautéed or roasted until very crisp and charred. This recipe does just that, with the welcome addition of some sweetness from the dried apricots.

1 garlic bulb
250 g/9 oz. Brussels sprouts, halved
400-g/14-oz. can of chickpeas/garbanzo beans, drained and rinsed
½ teaspoon cayenne pepper
3 tablespoons olive oil plus extra to drizzle
½ lemon, cut into wedges
80 g/½ cup dried apricots, halved
200 g/scant 1 cup natural yogurt
1 tablespoon harissa
sea salt and black pepper

SERVES 4

Preheat the oven to 200°C fan/220°C/425°F/Gas 7.

Separate the garlic bulb (but leave the individual cloves in their skins). Place the sprouts, chickpeas, garlic cloves, cayenne pepper, olive oil and some seasoning all on a large baking sheet. Squeeze over the lemon wedges, then add the wedges to the baking sheet. Using your hands, fold all of the ingredients into one another, to coat and combine.

Place the baking sheet on the top shelf of the preheated oven and roast for 25 minutes. Remove the baking sheet from the oven, add the apricot halves and fold through the roasted ingredients, then return to the oven for a final 5 minutes.

While the apricots get warmed up, mix the yogurt and harissa together, with a small drizzle of olive oil and a good pinch of seasoning. Spread the yogurt liberally over a serving dish, then once the roast items are ready and out of the oven, pile them on top of the yogurt and serve.

Sprout, cabbage & lettuce sauté

The perfect side dish, which goes particularly well with roast meats and/or fish dishes.

400 g/14 oz. Brussels sprouts
1 tablespoon olive oil
15 g/1 tablespoon butter
1 teaspoon caraway seeds
¼ green cabbage, thinly sliced
½ iceberg lettuce, cut into 1-cm/½-inch slices
juice of ½ lemon
½ teaspoon sea salt

SERVES 4–6

Separate as many leaves as you can from the Brussels sprouts and then thinly slice any remaining leaves that are too tight to separate. Set aside.

Heat a large sauté pan or wok. Add the oil and butter and heat to medium. Add the caraway seeds and sizzle for about 30 seconds. Add the sprouts and cabbage and stir-fry for about 4 minutes until wilted. Add the lettuce, stir-fry for a further minute, then quickly transfer to a serving dish. Pour over the lemon juice and sprinkle with the salt. Toss and serve immediately.

Creamy orzo with Brussels sprouts & sausages

Orzo is a small, barley-shaped pasta that has a natural affinity with cream and butter. This dish is an adaptation of a Nigel Slater recipes especially popular in autumn/fall and winter. Nigel recommends Italian-style sausages, seasoned with garlic and fennel seeds, but any sausage will work really.

200 g/7 oz. Brussels sprouts (about 12)
100 g/½ cup orzo
knob/pat of butter
1 tablespoon olive oil
3 sausages (about 200 g/7 oz.), sausagemeat removed from the skins
½–1 teaspoon dried mixed herbs or dried thyme
4 tablespoons dry Marsala or dry or medium sherry, plus extra if you wish
200 g/scant 1 cup crème fraîche
60 g/⅔ cup freshly grated Parmesan, plus extra to serve

SERVES 2

Trim the Brussels sprouts and halve any that are large. Cook in a generous amount of boiling salted water until tender – about 5 minutes. Drain in a colander placed over a bowl, reserving the cooking water.

Return the reserved water to the pan, bring to the boil and cook the orzo in it for the time recommended on the pack – orzo varies, from 6–10 minutes – drain and return to the pan. Stir in the butter to stop the orzo 'grains' sticking together.

Heat the oil in a large frying pan/skillet and fry the sausagemeat and herbs for 5–8 minutes until brown, breaking it up with a spatula into pieces no larger than bite-size and stirring frequently. Add the Marsala and stir well to deglaze the pan, then add the cooked sprouts and orzo, plus the crème fraîche and Parmesan, and heat through. Check the seasoning, add a splash more Marsala if you're in the mood, and serve with extra grated Parmesan.

Apple & cumin slaw with lime dressing

Here is a fresh, crunchy winter slaw that can be made in advance, and if you don't have an apple, try it with something else depending on what you have in the fruit bowl. The slaw will last a day or two in the fridge, but it will get softer and release more liquid.

1 teaspoon cumin seeds
250 g/9 oz. white or savoy cabbage
1 apple, cored (skin on)
grated zest and juice of 2 limes
80 g/⅓ cup Greek yogurt
1 garlic clove, grated
2 tablespoons cider vinegar
1 tablespoon wholegrain mustard
10 g/⅓ oz. fresh flat-leaf parsley, roughly chopped
sea salt and black pepper

SERVES 4 AS A SIDE

Add the cumin seeds to a frying pan/skillet set over a low-medium heat and lightly toast in the pan for 2–3 minutes, tossing often, until fragrant and slightly darkened in colour. Remove from the heat and let cool.

Finely shred the cabbage and thinly slice the apple and transfer to a mixing bowl. Douse in the lime zest and juice, tossing to coat the apple, then pile in the remaining ingredients, along with a good pinch of salt and pepper. Mix very well for about 3–4 minutes with your hands – really get in there! Finally, taste to check for seasoning.

Roasted red cabbage with charred broccoli, cherries & almonds

Red cabbage and broccoli roast beautifully and have an awesome affinity with sweet, tangy balsamic vinegar dressing. Plump juicy dried cherries and flaky almonds have been added for more flavour and crunch.

1 red cabbage
4 tablespoons olive oil
600 g/1 lb. 5 oz. broccoli
50 g/½ cup toasted, flaked/slivered almonds
100 g/¾ cup dried cherries
bunch of spring onions/scallions, chopped
large bunch of fresh dill, coarsely chopped
sea salt and black pepper

BALSAMIC DRESSING
3 tablespoons extra virgin olive oil
2 tablespoons balsamic vinegar
1 teaspoon caster/granulated sugar
sea salt flakes

SERVES 4

Preheat the oven to 200°C/180°C fan/400°F/gas 6. Cut the red cabbage into wedges and arrange them over a baking sheet. Drizzle with the oil, season and roast for 10 minutes. Chop the broccoli very finely – to an almost rice-like texture – and scatter it around the wedges of cabbage. Sprinkle with flaked almonds, return the pan to the oven and cook for a further 10 minutes.

Mix all the ingredients for the dressing together and season with salt flakes.

Remove the pan from the oven and gently push the cooked almonds into the broccoli using a fork. Drizzle everything with the dressing and scatter with the dried cherries, chopped spring onions and dill.

Charred hispi cabbage with juniper butter & crispy freekeh

When cabbage comes out of the oven, still with a little bite, its sweet flavour intensified against crisp, charred edges, you should prepare yourself for a treat.

1 hispi (pointed) cabbage, trimmed
4 tablespoons olive oil
250-g/9-oz. pouch pre-cooked freekeh
grated zest and juice of 1 lemon
sea salt and black pepper
chopped fresh flat-leaf parsley, to garnish

JUNIPER BUTTER
100 g/½ cup butter, softened
20 juniper berries
1 generous teaspoon chopped fresh rosemary
50 g/1¾ oz. dried cherries, roughly chopped

SERVES 3–4

Place the butter in a bowl. Crush the juniper berries using a pestle and mortar. Add the juniper, rosemary and dried cherries to the bowl, and work everything together with a fork until evenly mixed.

Lay a piece of cling film/plastic wrap on a clean work surface. Form the butter into a small sausage shape, and roll up in the cling film. Give the package a little roll backwards and forwards to create an even shape and swizzle the ends to seal. Transfer to the fridge to firm up.

Preheat the oven to 190°C/170°C fan/375°F/gas 5. Cut the cabbage in half from root to tip, then cut each half into three or four wedges. Arrange them on a baking sheet and drizzle with half of the oil. Bake for 10 minutes.

Remove the pan from the oven, scatter over the freekeh and drizzle over the remaining olive oil. Return to the oven and cook for a further 5 minutes or so until the freekeh is hot and crisp and the edges of the cabbage are lightly charred. Remove from the oven, scatter over the lemon zest and juice, season with salt and black pepper and garnish with freshly chopped parsley. Serve while hot, with thin slices of the juniper and cherry butter melting into the leaves.

Shaved broccoli & buckwheat salad with dukkah topping

This salad uses the forgotten broccoli stems that can be quite attractive shaved into strips and is a great way of making the use of the whole vegetable. Buckwheat, one of our great supergrains, is nice for this, but wheatberries would be just as good for those who are avoiding gluten. Dukkah is a special addition to any salad. It is made up of crushed seeds, nuts and spices that are tasty and great for digestion.

240 ml/1 cup vegetable stock
185 g/1 cup buckwheat groats
4 broccoli stalks
15 g/⅛ cup chopped hazelnuts

DRESSING
300 g/1⅓ cups natural/plain yogurt
juice of 2 lemons
½ teaspoon sea salt
½ teaspoon cumin powder
a bunch of fresh coriander/cilantro, chopped

DUKKAH TOPPING
2 teaspoons cumin seeds
2 teaspoons coriander seeds
1 teaspoon fennel seeds
100 g/¾ cup roasted hazelnuts
100 g/¾ cup roasted sunflower seeds
1 teaspoon sea salt

SERVES 4–6

In a large saucepan or pot, put the vegetable stock, buckwheat groats and 240 ml/1 cup water over a medium–high heat. Bring to the boil, then turn down the heat and simmer for 15 minutes with the lid half on, stirring once half way through. Be careful not to overcook the groats. Drain and rinse with cold water then set aside in a bowl to cool.

Peel and shave the broccoli stalks into ribbons using a vegetable peeler or mandoline then add to a large saucepan or pot of boiling water. Cook for 3 minutes, then shock the broccoli to suspend the cooking by submerging it in a bowl of iced water. Drain, cool and mix with the hazelnuts and reserved buckwheat.

For the dressing, whisk all the ingredients together and store in the refrigerator until you are ready to serve.

For the dukkah topping, use a pestle and mortar to grind the cumin, coriander and fennel seeds by hand. Blend the hazelnuts and sunflower seeds in a food processor to a roughly chopped consistency. Mix in a bowl with the crushed spices then set aside. This should yield about 200 g/ 1½ cups of dukkah.

To serve, spoon the broccoli and buckwheat mix onto individual plates, drizzle over the dressing and cover each serving with a tablespoon of dukkah topping.

Purple sprouting broccoli & flageolet beans with preserved lemon mayo

This easy-peasy combo of crispy, lightly charred broccoli, soft garlicky beans, crunchy lemony crumbs and zippy, unctuous preserved lemon mayo makes a fabulous light lunch.

350 g/12 oz. purple sprouting broccoli
400-g/14-oz. can flageolet beans, drained and rinsed
3 tablespoons olive oil
2 garlic cloves, finely chopped
large handful of fresh parsley, finely chopped
3 tablespoons panko crumbs
grated zest of 1 lemon

LEMON MAYO
1 egg
1 garlic clove, grated
1 tablespoon Dijon mustard
juice of ½ lemon
250 ml/1 cup sunflower oil
¼–½ preserved lemon

SERVES 4

To make the preserved lemon mayo, put the egg, grated garlic, mustard and lemon juice into a jug/pitcher. Whiz everything together using a handheld stick blender. Slowly add the oil, keeping the blender going and pouring in a steady stream, until all the oil is incorporated and the mixture is thick and light. Rinse the salt from the preserved lemon, remove the inner flesh and discard. Finely chop the softened skin and add it to the mayonnaise. Cover and refrigerate until ready to use.

Preheat the oven to 180°C/160°C fan/350°F/gas 4.

Trim the broccoli. Leave the stalks quite long, but peel away any tough bits using a vegetable peeler. Lay the broccoli over a baking sheet and cook for 10–15 minutes until the broccoli is al dente, but starting to crisp.

Pop the beans into a bowl and add the oil, garlic and parsley. Remove the broccoli from the oven and spoon the beans over. Mix the panko crumbs and lemon zest together and scatter this over the top. Return the baking sheet to the oven and cook for a further 5 minutes until the beans are warmed through. Take care not to leave the pan in for too long, or the beans will dry and crack. Serve with the preserved lemon mayo.

Chicken & broccoli one-pan pasta

Who doesn't love a creamy pasta partnered with torn chicken and fresh greens? Feel free to change up the ingredients here based on what you have lurking in the fridge or freezer and needs using up, there are so many alternatives and combinations.

200 g/7 oz. cooked chicken
2 garlic cloves, thinly sliced
900 ml/4 scant cups boiling water
1 chicken stock pot
160 g/5½ oz. dried pasta
100 g/¾ cup frozen peas
200 g/7 oz. Tenderstem broccoli/broccolini, stems sliced into 3–4 pieces
150 g/¾ cup crème fraîche
juice of 1 lemon
30 g/⅓ cup grated Parmesan
10 g/⅓ oz. fresh mint, stalks discarded
olive oil, for cooking
sea salt and black pepper

SERVES 2

Add a drizzle of oil to a large, high-sided frying pan/skillet set over a medium heat. When hot, add the chicken and garlic and fry for 5 minutes, stirring very often to avoid the garlic burning. Next, add the water, stock pot and pasta to the pan with a generous pinch of seasoning. Bring to the boil, cover with a lid and let bubble away for 8 minutes.

When there are only 4 minutes of cooking time left, add the greens (peas and broccoli), stir in and replace the lid. You might need to increase the heat slightly to get the temperature back up to a good bubble. Add a splash more water if the pasta is looking in need. After 4 minutes, remove the lid and reduce the heat to low, then add the crème fraîche and stir in. Taste to check for seasoning. Remove the pan from the heat and add the lemon juice, Parmesan and mint leaves. Stir well, then pile into bowls, making sure you pour all the soupy sauce in too. Finish with extra Parmesan if you like.

Broccoli pesto

Make this pesto with that last crown of broccoli haunting your salad drawer. It's so versatile and can be used to mix into pasta or drizzled over soup, grilled meats or fish.

1 small head of broccoli (including stems), chopped into small pieces
1 garlic clove
30 g/1 oz. fresh basil
3–4 tablespoons olive oil
½ teaspoon nutritional yeast
¼ teaspoon salt, plus more to taste

MAKES ABOUT 350 ML/1½ CUPS

Cook the broccoli in a steamer basket or in a covered pan with a little boiling water for 3–5 minutes until tender. Drain and run under cold water. Combine the broccoli with the remaining ingredients in a small food processor and blend until smooth-ish. Adjust the seasoning to taste.

Seriously cheesy cauliflower

Once you've made this you might decide never to make conventional cauliflower cheese again. This method is courtesy of Tom Kerridge. *Pictured on page 137.*

1 small cauliflower, trimmed
½ teaspoon ground turmeric
freshly grated nutmeg
200 ml/¾ cup double/heavy cream
175 g/3 generous cups grated cheese (Cheddar, Gruyère, soft cheeses, or a mixture, basically whatever you have to hand)
2 tablespoons freshly grated Parmesan
black pepper

SERVES 2

Cut yourself a square of baking parchment and two squares of foil large enough to enclose the cauliflower.

Place the cauliflower on the baking parchment and sprinkle with the turmeric and nutmeg and generous seasoning. Wrap tightly, then wrap again in the first sheet of foil, then the second, patting it on snugly. Put on a baking sheet and bake at 210°C/190°C fan/425°F/gas 7 for 1–1¼ hours until completely cooked. Test by jabbing a knife right through the foil package, and make a final check by unwrapping. (There is no need to preheat the oven, but leave it on for step 5.)

Meanwhile, put the cream in a pan and bubble gently for 4–5 minutes until slightly thickened. Season well and stir in the cheese.

Taking care not to burn yourself, transfer the cauliflower to an oval dish and slice in quarters down the centre. Sprinkle the cut surfaces with the cheese mixture and finish with the Parmesan.

Return to the oven for 10–12 minutes, rotating the dish at half time so it cooks evenly, until the cheese has melted and is beginning to turn brown in spots. Leave to cool for 5–10 minutes before serving with a grinding of black pepper, if liked.

Cauliflower steak sandwiches

An unexpectedly delicious vegetarian sandwich. Perfect as part of a lunch spread, where they can be served sliced in half with a big salad on the side.

1 medium head of cauliflower
120 ml/½ cup red wine vinegar
2 teaspoons coconut or cane sugar
½ teaspoon salt
1 red onion, sliced into thin half-moons
1 carrot, peeled into ribbons
25 g/¼ cup black olives, stoned/pitted and torn
3 tablespoons chopped fresh flat-leaf parsley leaves
1 tablespoon capers, drained (optional)

TO SERVE
8 slices of sourdough bread
chipotle or sriracha mayonnaise
Cos/Romaine lettuce leaves
crumbled feta (optional)

a baking sheet, greased with a thin layer of olive oil

SERVES 4

Preheat the oven to 220°C/200°C fan/425°F/gas 7.

Working from the centre outwards, slice the head of cauliflower into 2.5–4 cm/1–1½-inch pieces (these should look like the cross section of the entire head of cauliflower). Don't worry if they crumble a bit.

Arrange the cauliflower 'steaks' on the prepared baking sheet and roast in the preheated oven for 25 minutes. Flip each piece with a spatula and return to oven for 10 minutes until golden and tender.

Meanwhile, in a medium bowl, combine the vinegar, sugar and salt with 120 ml/½ cup of water. Toss the onion and carrot in the pickling liquid and set aside for at least 20 minutes.

To serve, drain the onion and carrot and combine in a bowl with the olives, parsley and capers (if using). Spread the bread with creamy chipotle mayo, top with a cauliflower steak and the carrot mixture. Finish the sandwiches with a crisp rib of lettuce and a little feta (if using).

Cauliflower & cherry tomato bake with grilled halloumi

A colourful vegetable-based supper dish. Use a medium-sized roasting tin or baking sheet. While the potatoes are in the oven, prepare the cauliflower, chickpeas, garlic, tomatoes and crushed chillies/hot red pepper flakes, piling them all into a bowl, ready for the whole lot to be tipped in to the pan in step 2.

250 g/9 oz. new potatoes, halved
1 red onion, cut into wedges
1 orange (bell) pepper, deseeded and sliced
1 tablespoon olive oil
½ small cauliflower, broken into small florets
½ a 400-g/14-oz. can chickpeas/garbanzo beans, drained and rinsed
2 garlic cloves, thinly sliced
125 g/4½ oz. cherry tomatoes
good pinch of crushed chillies/hot pepper flakes
½ a 250-g/9-oz. block of halloumi, sliced
2 tablespoons toasted walnuts

SERVES 2

Put the potatoes, onion and pepper in a roasting pan, toss with the oil and seasoning and roast at 180°C/160°C fan/350°F/gas 4 for 25–30 minutes until the potatoes are beginning to soften. Stir halfway through. (There is no need to preheat your oven but it will save you 5 minutes if you do.)

Stir in all the remaining ingredients, except the halloumi and walnuts, season well and return to the oven to bake for another 30 minutes until brown and tender.

Preheat the grill/broiler about 5 minutes before you wish to eat. Pat the halloumi slices dry with kitchen paper towels and lay it on the surface of the vegetables. Grill/broil for 4–6 minutes until the halloumi is golden.

Top with the toasted walnuts and eat while the halloumi is still hot.

Cauliflower masala

In this simple masala, cauliflower is stir-fried in a seasoned, spiced oil until just tender.

1 tablespoon sunflower oil
2 teaspoons cumin seeds
1 teaspoon black mustard seeds
500 g/1 lb. 2oz. cauliflower florets
2 garlic cloves, sliced
2 teaspoons finely chopped fresh ginger
1 green chilli/chile, sliced
1 teaspoon garam masala
150 ml/⅔ cup hot water
juice of ½ lemon
sea salt and black pepper

SERVES 4

Heat the sunflower oil in a large frying pan/skillet over a medium heat. Add the cumin seeds and mustard seeds. Stir-fry for 30 seconds, then add the cauliflower, garlic, ginger and chilli. Turn the heat to high and stir-fry for 6–8 minutes, or until the cauliflower is lightly browned at the edges. Stir in the garam masala and hot water and stir well. Cover and cook over a high heat for 1–2 minutes. Season well and drizzle with the lemon juice just before serving.

Summer & Winter Squash

PUMPKIN | SQUASH | COURGETTES

Miso & umeboshi baked pumpkin with quick asparagus & carrot kimchi

A vegetable-centric dish worthy of the main event! This roasted pumpkin is delicious served on bread or a savoury pancake with some kimchi and a spoonful of Japanese mayonnaise.

1 kabocha pumpkin or 3 small pumpkins
bunch of spring onions/scallions
4 tablespoons flavourless oil
2 teaspoons sesame oil
4 tablespoons white miso paste
2 tablespoons soy sauce
4 tablespoons mirin
4 teaspoons umeboshi paste

TO SERVE
Quick asparagus & carrot kimchi (see below)
Japanese mayo

cooking string (optional)
roasting pan, lined with baking parchment

SERVES 4–5

Preheat the oven to 180°C/160°C fan/350°F/gas 4.

Cut the pumpkin(s) in half lengthways and deseed. Cut the pumpkin(s) into 5-cm/2-inch thick wedges and tie loosely together with cooking string. Nestle the spring onions between the wedges and place in the prepared roasting pan. (Alternatively, you can spread the wedges and onions in a roasting pan without tying.)

Mix together the remaining ingredients in a small bowl with 2 tablespoons water to make a marinade and brush generously all over the pumpkin slices.

Roast in the preheated oven for 30–40 minutes for 1 medium pumpkin (or 30–35 minutes for 3 smaller pumpkins), turning over halfway through, until tender. Shake the pan to coat the pumpkin pieces in the sticky marinade before serving with the kimchi below.

Quick asparagus & carrot kimchi

200 g/7 oz. asparagus, shaved into ribbons
200 g/7 oz. carrots, peeled and shaved into ribbons
1 tablespoon sea salt
1 tablespoon sugar
5 spring onions/scallions, cut into 5-cm/2-inch lengths
1 tablespoon gochugaru (coarse Korean chilli/chili pepper) or 1 tablespoon chilli flakes/hot red pepper flakes, finely ground
2 garlic cloves, crushed
1 tablespoon fish sauce
1 thumb-sized piece of fresh ginger, peeled and grated

SERVES 4–5

In a large bowl, toss together the asparagus, carrots, salt and sugar.

Add the spring onions, gochugaru (or chilli flakes), garlic, fish sauce, and ginger and toss well to coat.

Serve immediately or cover with cling film/plastic wrap and leave at room temperature for 2 days to allow fermentation to begin before refrigerating. This kimchi will keep for only a few days in the fridge as it is a quick version.

Thai vegetable curry

This is an easy weeknight curry that really celebrates vegetables. It's easy, full of colour and you can make it ahead and reheat over a low heat when you're ready to eat.

coconut or avocado oil, for frying
1 onion, finely diced
1 yellow (bell) pepper, deseeded and chopped into thin strips
1 tablespoon grated fresh ginger
1 tablespoon chopped fresh coriander/cilantro stems (leaves reserved for serving)
2 tablespoons red Thai curry paste, or more to taste
235 ml/1 cup vegetable stock
250 g/2 cups kabocha pumpkin or butternut squash, peeled and cut into 1.5-cm/½-inch chunks
400-g/14-oz. can coconut milk
1 tablespoon tamari
1 head of broccoli, cut into small florets
130 g/1 cup frozen shelled edamame beans or peas, thawed
sea salt
cooked brown rice or quinoa, to serve (optional)

SERVES 4

Heat a thin layer of oil in a large saucepan over a medium-high heat. Add the onion, pepper and a pinch of salt and cook for 5 minutes, stirring occasionally.

Add the ginger, coriander stems and curry paste and cook, stirring, for 1 minute. Add the vegetable stock and the pumpkin and stir to combine. Reduce the heat to medium, cover with a lid and cook for 7–8 minutes.

Stir in the coconut milk, tamari, broccoli and edamame beans or peas, cover with a lid and bring to the boil. Reduce the heat and simmer for another 3–5 minutes until the butternut squash and broccoli are tender and easily pierced with a fork. Remove from the heat and allow to stand for 5 minutes uncovered.

Taste for seasoning, adding more salt if needed, and serve warm over cooked rice or quinoa (if desired) and top with fresh coriander to serve.

Baking sheet pizza with pesto winter squash

Pizza is the ultimate laid-back, sharing food that brings people together. You will need to make the dough for this one a day in advance, but the upside is, it doesn't require any kneading. It's the perfect vehicle for deeply roasted squash.

PIZZA DOUGH
500 g/3¾ cups '00' flour, plus extra for shaping
¾ teaspoon active dry yeast
2 teaspoons fine sea salt

PESTO SQUASH TOPPING
1 winter squash (such as delicata), seeds removed and sliced into 1.5-cm/½-inch thick pieces
1 red onion, sliced into 1.5 cm/½-inch thick wedges
olive oil, for drizzling
1 whole head of garlic, base cut off to expose cloves but still attached
100 g/½ cup Broccoli Pesto (see page 134 or store bought)
2 tablespoons olive oil
115 g/½ cup ricotta (optional)
2 large handfuls of rocket/arugula
4–6 leaves of radicchio, thinly sliced
sea salt

large baking sheet and a 46 x 33-cm/18 x 13-inch baking sheet, both oiled

MAKES 2 PIZZAS

Make the dough a day in advance. Use a fork to mix together the flour, yeast and salt in a large mixing bowl. Slowly add 350 ml/1½ cups of water and mix together with your hands until just combined into a ball. Cover the bowl with a clean kitchen cloth and rest the dough in a warm room for at least 18 and up to 24 hours until doubled in size.

For the pizza topping, preheat the oven to 200°C/180°C fan/400°F/ gas 6. Arrange the squash and onion on the first prepared baking sheet and season with salt. Drizzle a square of foil with a little oil and use this to wrap the head of garlic into a parcel. Put the parcel on the sheet with the squash and roast in the preheated oven for 25 minutes until tender. When cool, remove the soft garlic pulp from its skin and set aside.

Punch the pizza dough down a little to deflate it. Dust a clean work surface with flour, tip out the dough and cut in half. Slowly stretch one of the balls of dough into a rectangle with your hands and put on the second prepared baking sheet. Continue to stretch the dough until it almost fits the size of the baking sheet. Patch any major holes in the dough, but don't worry about making it perfect, it should be fairly thin though.

Preheat the oven to its highest setting. Position the oven rack in the middle.

Mix the pesto with the 2 tablespoons oil and spread half across the dough. Put the pizza in the oven, then lower the heat to 230°C/210°C fan/ 450°F/ gas 8. Bake for 12–15 minutes until starting to turn golden at the edges. Remove from the oven.

Preheat the grill/broiler. Top the pizza with half the roasted garlic cloves, lightly squashing them with a fork. If using ricotta, dollop teaspoons of half across the dough. Scatter half the roasted squash and onions on the pizza.

Grill/broil for 2 minutes and remove when browned in places – watch carefully to make sure it doesn't burn. Your dough should be cooked through and mostly golden. Top with half the rocket and radicchio. Cool for 5 minutes, then cut into squares. Repeat with the other half of the dough and remaining ingredients.

Winter vegetable bowl

Winter can be rough on veggie lovers, when farm fresh tomatoes and juicy stone fruit seem another world away. Here's a bowl that celebrates cold weather produce and perks it up with a tasty lemon and olive chermoula and crunchy toasted walnuts.

130 g/¾ cup wild rice
1 acorn squash, sliced in half and seeds removed, then sliced into thin half-moons
1 red onion, cut into wedges
1–2 tablespoons avocado or olive oil
300 g/3 cups Brussels sprouts, woody bases and outer leaves removed, then thinly sliced (so you get ribbons of Brussels sprouts leaves)
2 big handfuls of baby rocket/arugula or spinach
sea salt and black pepper
shop-bought pesto, tapenade or chermoula, to serve
50 g/⅓ cup toasted walnuts, roughly chopped, to serve

baking sheet, lightly greased with olive oil

SERVES 3–4

Preheat the oven to 220°C/200°C fan/425°F/gas 7.

In a medium saucepan, combine the wild rice with 350 ml/1½ cups of water. Cover with a lid and bring to a boil. Add a pinch of salt, reduce the heat to medium-low and simmer for about 40 minutes, or according to the package instructions, until the rice is cooked.

Meanwhile, arrange the squash and onion on the oiled baking sheet. Roast in the preheated oven for about 25–30 minutes, rotating the sheet and flipping the veg half-way through.

Meanwhile, heat the oil in a large saucepan or a frying pan/skillet with high sides over a medium-high heat. Add the shredded Brussels sprouts and sprinkle with a good pinch of salt. Cook, stirring a few times, for about 5 minutes until the sprouts are softened; they should be mostly bright green but golden in places. Stir in the rocket or spinach and remove from the heat. Taste and add salt and pepper as desired.

To assemble the bowls, start with a scoop of rice and top with lots of Brussels sprouts, roasted squash and red onion. Add a generous drizzle of pesto, tapenade or chermoula and walnuts to finish.

Roast butternut squash with lentils, pomegranates & pine nuts

Roasting the squash in its skin gives the whole vegetable such a fabulous texture and the skin is unbelievably good to eat. Serve with a rocket/arugula salad.

2 small butternut squash, halved and deseeded
4–5 tablespoons olive oil
handful of fresh thyme leaves
2 tablespoons chopped fresh rosemary
2 large leeks, trimmed and chopped
300 g/10½ oz. baby plum tomatoes
400-g/14-oz. can black beluga lentils
50 g/scant ½ cup toasted pine nuts
handful of pomegranate seeds
sea salt and black pepper

DRESSING
3½ tablespoons olive oil
3½ tablespoons pomegranate molasses, plus extra to serve

SERVES 4

Preheat the oven to 190°C/170°C fan/375°F/gas 5. Lightly score a diamond pattern into the flesh of the squash using the tip of a sharp knife. Drizzle with a little of the oil, sprinkle with the thyme and rosemary, place on a baking sheet and bake for 15 minutes. Remove the baking sheet from the oven and push the squash over to one side. Scatter the chopped leeks and whole baby plum tomatoes on the other side of the baking sheet and drizzle with the remaining oil. Scatter with salt and freshly ground black pepper and return to the oven for another 20 minutes until the flesh of the squash is soft and the leeks and tomatoes are lightly charred. Scoop the leeks and tomatoes into a large bowl.

Drain and rinse the lentils, and add them to the bowl. Mix the olive oil and pomegranate molasses together for the dressing and add about half to the lentil mixture. Pile the mixture into the squash hollows and return the sheet pan to the oven. Bake for 5 minutes, until the lentil filling is just heated through.

Remove from the oven, drizzle over the remaining dressing, scatter with the pine nuts and pomegranate seeds. Add a good grinding of black pepper.

Spaghetti with squash, sage & pecorino

This tasty pasta is inspired by the classic Italian dish of pumpkin-filled ravioli with sage butter, except this is an inside-out version and therefore much easier to make.

65 ml/¼ cup light olive oil
400 g/14 oz. butternut squash, deseeded and cut into wedges
2 garlic cloves, chopped
10–12 small fresh sage leaves
400 g/14 oz. spaghetti
handful of flat-leaf parsley, chopped
50 g/½ cup grated Pecorino cheese
sea salt and black pepper

SERVES 4

Put the oil in a frying pan/skillet and set over a high heat. Add the squash and cook for 5–6 minutes, turning often, until golden but not breaking up. Add the garlic and sage to the pan and cook for 2–3 minutes. Remove from the heat and let sit to allow the flavours to develop.

Cook the pasta according to the packet instructions. Drain well and return to the warm pan with the squash mixture. Add the parsley and half of the Pecorino and season well with salt and pepper. Serve immediately with the remaining cheese sprinkled over the top.

Roasted marrow & courgette pasta

Even if you don't have your own vegetable patch, you probably know someone who has one and ends up with a glut of marrow and courgettes/zucchini every year! One of my favourite ways to use it is this simple, creamy pasta sauce. You need to have tender, pre-roasted marrow before you start for the best results.

200 g/7 oz. dried pasta
1 onion, thinly sliced
1 courgette/zucchini, thinly sliced
150 g/5½ oz. pre-roasted marrow (see Tip below), roughly chopped
1 teaspoon garlic purée
100 ml/⅓ cup whole milk
1 teaspoon Dijon mustard
juice of 1 lemon
sea salt and black pepper
olive oil, for frying
grated Pecorino and extra virgin olive oil, to serve

SERVES 2

Fill a large saucepan with water and season very well. Bring to the boil, then add the pasta and cook according to packet instructions.

Add a glug of olive oil to a large, non-stick frying pan/skillet set over a medium heat. Add the onion to the pan, letting it sizzle for 15 minutes, gently frying and caramelizing. Stir often to avoid burning.

Add the courgette and fry for 3 minutes, stirring often. Next, add the marrow and garlic and fry for another 2 minutes. Add the milk and mustard to the pan and let bubble for about 3 minutes, stirring almost constantly, until you have a gloopy, lumpy, sloppy but delicious sauce in the pan. Squeeze in half the lemon juice and taste to check for seasoning. Remove the sauce from the heat if the pasta is still cooking.

When the pasta is ready, reserve a mug of pasta cooking water, then drain. Tip the pasta into the sauce and pour in a splash of pasta water too. Put back on the heat and bring to a gentle simmer, stir or toss to combine well. If you think it's looking a bit dry, add a splash more pasta water. Taste to check for seasoning and add more lemon juice, salt and pepper to your taste. Pile into bowls and top with some Pecorino, then add a final drizzle of olive oil before serving.

TIPS

- *To roast marrow, it should be washed and cut into cubes or wedges first. Preheat the oven to 190°C/170°C fan/375°F/gas 5. Place the marrow in a roasting dish, drizzle with oil and season with salt and pepper. Bake in the preheated oven for 45 minutes, giving the marrow a toss every 15 minutes or so, until soft and lightly golden.*
- *To make into a pasta bake, add a little more milk to the leftovers to loosen up, then top with breadcrumbs, soft herbs and grated cheese (mix them up) and bake in a hot oven.*

Roasted vegetable & orecchiette salad with a tomato & caper dressing

This is the easiest most versatile pasta salad. In fact it's a hybrid – it can be eaten as a hot pasta dish, which is sweet and sour with the tomato caper dressing, with loads of cheese or allowed to cool and be eaten as a side salad, perfect for a barbecue.

300 g/10½ oz. orecchiette pasta
1 large aubergine/eggplant, cut into 5-mm/¼-in. slices
1 courgette/zucchini, cut into 5-mm/¼-in. slices
1 yellow (bell) pepper, cut into 5-mm/¼-in. strips
3 garlic cloves
3 tablespoons olive oil
2 tablespoons sultanas/golden raisins
small bunch of fresh basil, leaves picked
2 handfuls of rocket/arugula
grated zest of ½ lemon (juice reserved for dressing)
2 tablespoons pine nuts
20 g/¾ oz. Pecorino, shaved
sea salt and black pepper

TOMATO CAPER DRESSING
4 tablespoons Simple Summer Tomato Sauce (see page 67)
2 teaspoons capers, drained and chopped
juice of ½ lemon
1 tablespoon balsamic vinegar
5 tablespoons olive oil

SERVES 4

Preheat the oven to 220°C/200°C fan/425°F/gas 7.

Cook the pasta following the packet instructions. Drain and rinse under cold running water until cool, then drain again.

Place all the vegetables in a roasting pan with the garlic and drizzle with the oil. Season well with salt and pepper. Roast the vegetables in the preheated oven for 20 minutes. Toss everything together and return to the oven for a further 5–10 minutes, or until hot. Remove from the oven and leave to cool.

In a bowl, mix the dressing ingredients and taste for seasoning. Place the dressing in the base of a serving bowl, add the cooked pasta and roasted vegetables and mix through the dressing. Top with the sultanas, basil, rocket, lemon zest, pine nuts and Pecorino.

Fregola with courgettes, corn, basil & ricotta

Sometimes called Sardinian couscous, fregola lands somewhere between a grain and a pasta, with a nutty flavour. It works beautifully with the fresh courgettes/zucchini here.

200 g/7 oz. fregola
3 tablespoons olive oil
1 shallot, finely chopped
2 courgettes/zucchini, sliced
3 garlic cloves, crushed
pinch of Aleppo chilli/hot red pepper flakes
2 corn on the cob, kernels shaved
30 g/1 oz. Manchego, shaved, plus extra to garnish
15–20 fresh basil leaves, plus extra to garnish
grated zest and juice of 1 lemon
sea salt and black pepper

RICOTTA
250-g/9-oz. block of ricotta
2 tablespoons olive oil
1 tablespoon runny honey
1 teaspoon dried oregano
1 teaspoon Aleppo chilli/hot red pepper flakes

SERVES 4

Cook the fregola in a large saucepan of boiling water according to the packet instructions, then drain and set aside to cool, reserving about 250 ml/1 cup of the cooking water.

Heat 2 tablespoons of the oil in a large griddle/grill pan or sauté pan over a medium heat. Add the shallot and courgettes and some salt and pepper and cook for a few minutes. Add the garlic and chilli flakes and cook for a few more minutes until the garlic is fragrant. Add the corn and continue sautéing for 5–6 minutes until the corn is tender, but still a little snappy.

Add the cooked fregola to the courgette mixture, drizzle with another tablespoon of olive oil and stir in the Manchego, basil and lemon zest. Add 60–120 ml/¼–½ cup of the pasta water to loosen, and more if you prefer it more 'saucy'. Garnish with fresh basil and an extra sprinkling of Manchego.

Place the block of ricotta on a serving dish and drizzle with olive oil and runny honey, then finish with the oregano and chilli flakes. Serve alongside the fregola with courgettes, placing a few tablespoons into the mixture or letting guests help themselves.

Honey-roasted courgettes with feta

The courgette/zucchini has many wonderful uses – both cooked and raw (try them grated into salads), savoury and sweet. Here, they are roasted until deeply golden and unctuous.

500 g/1 lb. 2 oz. courgettes/zucchini, cut into chunky batons
2 garlic cloves, sliced
3 tablespoons extra virgin olive oil
200 g/7 oz. feta cheese, crumbled
2 tablespoons runny honey
black pepper

SERVES 4

Preheat the oven to 220°C/200°C fan/425°F/gas 7. Put the courgettes into a large ovenproof dish in a single layer. Add the garlic and sprinkle with 2 tablespoons of the olive oil. Using your hands, toss the courgettes until they are evenly coated with the garlic and oil. Spread out the courgettes evenly in the dish. Scatter the feta over them and trickle with the remaining olive oil, honey and pepper. Roast in the preheated oven until deep golden. Transfer to a serving dish and serve immediately.

Mushrooms & Fungi

DRIED & FRESH MUSHROOMS

Dried mushroom risotto

This is a super simple, pared-back risotto that allows the dried mushrooms to pump some umami and depth into the dish. As always with a risotto, make sure you season well – the starch needs it. The best part of making a risotto is adding the cold butter and Parmesan at the end, so take a minute to enjoy watching what happens in the pan as you do. A moment of meditative joy!

1.5 litres/6¼ cups chicken stock
20 g/¾ oz. dried mushrooms
knob/pat of unsalted butter
1 large onion, finely chopped
3 garlic cloves, grated
350 g/1¾ cups risotto rice
3½ tablespoons white wine
1 lemon
20 g/1½ tablespoons salted butter, fridge cold
50 g/½ cup grated Parmesan, plus extra to serve
sea salt and black pepper

SERVES 4

Add the stock and dried mushrooms to a saucepan and bring to the boil. Once boiling, reduce the heat to very low and keep on the heat, not simmering, just hot. Pop a ladle in the pan so you're ready to go.

Add a knob/pat of butter to a wide-bottomed saucepan and once hot, add the onion and fry gently for 10 minutes until softened.

Meanwhile, peel and grate the garlic. Once the onions have had their time, add the garlic and fry for 2 minutes, stirring often to avoid burning, then add the risotto rice. Mix well for a minute or so to coat the grains in the butter, then add the wine and let bubble away until most of the liquid has been absorbed.

Add the first ladle of chicken and mushroom stock, and let the risotto gently bubble, stirring often. Once the liquid has been almost completely absorbed, add another ladle of stock. Settle the temperature to a gentle simmer, and once that ladleful has been almost completely absorbed again, add a third. Continue with this process until the risotto rice is almost al dente – this should take about 20 minutes.

When the rice is almost ready, season, taste and season again (remembering you're about to add Parmesan though, so don't go too mad on the salt).

Remove the pan from the heat, then add a final, scant ladleful of stock (scooping up any now-soft mushroom pieces still in the pan of stock). Grate the lemon zest into the risotto, then halve the lemon and add a squeeze of juice to the pan too. Also add the cold butter and Parmesan. Stir well, enjoy watching the butter and cheese melt and turn the risotto into velvety heaven. Taste to check for seasoning one final time, then pile onto plates immediately. Cut the remaining lemon half into wedges and take to the table, along with the Parmesan.

Linguine with porcini, pecorino & marsala

Precious porcini mushrooms, so beloved by the Italians, are sold dried and sliced. Only a few slices are needed to give an extra umami boost to dishes such as risottos, soups or stews, and are often used in conjunction with fresh mushrooms, as has been done here with this creamy, garlicky pasta dish.

- about 16 g/½ oz. dried porcini mushrooms
- 1 tablespoon olive oil
- 15 g/1 tablespoon butter
- 250 g/9 oz. portabello mushrooms, sliced about 2 cm/¾ inch thick
- 1 garlic clove, crushed
- 125 g/½ cup mascarpone, cream cheese or double/heavy cream
- 4 tablespoons dry Marsala, plus extra to serve
- 60 g/⅔ cup freshly grated Pecorino Romano or Parmesan, plus extra to serve
- 200–250 g/7–9 oz. (depending on appetite) dried linguine
- 4 tablespoons soured cream (optional)

SERVES 2

Put the porcini in a small bowl and fill with boiling water. Leave for 10 minutes, then drain in a small sieve/strainer and, using your fingers, rinse well under the tap (to remove any vestigial grit), lightly squeeze dry and chop roughly.

Heat the oil and butter in a large frying pan/skillet and fry the soaked porcini and portabello mushrooms with plenty of seasoning for 6–minutes until juicy and shiny and any exuded liquid has boiled away. Add the garlic and sizzle gently for 30 seconds.

Stir in the mascarpone and Marsala and simmer gently until heated through and slightly thickened, then stir in the cheese and keep warm.

Cook the pasta according to packet instructions until al dente, drain and stir into the sauce. Taste and add a touch more Marsala, if you wish. Serve topped with a dollop of soured cream, if liked, and more grated cheese.

Three-mushroom goulash

This tasty and substantial supper dish can be served with boiled potatoes (in the Hungarian style), rice or tagliatelle: if you have poppy seeds to hand, sprinkle on lightly to provide a soft crunch. Feel free to halve the quantity of tomatoes and add a small glass of red wine, if liked.

8 g/¼ oz. dried porcini mushrooms
300 g/10½ oz. mixed fresh mushrooms
splash of olive oil
15 g/1 tablespoon butter
1 shallot, sliced
1 tablespoon tomato purée/paste
1 garlic clove, crushed
1 teaspoon smoked paprika, plus extra to garnish
½ teaspoon caraway seeds, lightly crushed
230-g/8 oz. can chopped tomatoes, or ½ a 400-g/14-oz. can
splash of water, wine or stock, if necessary
squeeze of lemon juice
200-g/7-oz. tub soured cream
sea salt and black pepper
chopped fresh flat-leaf parsley or tarragon, to serve

SERVES 2

Put the porcini in a cup or heatproof bowl, cover with 100 ml/⅓ cup boiling water and set aside to steep while you trim the mushrooms. Slice any large mushrooms, halve or quarter smaller ones, but aim for a variety of shapes and sizes. Now line a small sieve/strainer with a piece of kitchen paper towel and place over a cup or jug/pitcher. Fish the porcini out of their soaking liquid (do not discard) with your fingers, rinse under the tap to remove any remaining grit and slice roughly. Pour the soaking juices into the sieve, allow the liquid to filter through and discard the kitchen paper towel and the bits caught in it.

Heat the oil and butter in a large frying pan /skillet and add the shallot. Cook over a medium heat until starting to go brown – 2–3 minutes – then raise the heat and add the mushrooms and porcini. Some mushrooms release water, so just keep stirring and sizzling until any liquid has boiled away and the mushrooms are appealingly browned, about 5 minutes. Stir in the tomato purée, garlic, paprika and caraway and cook for 30 seconds.

Now stir in the porcini soaking juices and tomatoes and simmer for about 5 minutes until slightly thickened. Add a splash of water, wine or stock if necessary, to achieve a saucy consistency. Season well and add a squeeze of lemon juice to brighten the flavour.

When ready to serve, swirl in about three-quarters of the soured cream and heat through. Check the seasoning and serve with the remaining soured cream and a sprinkle of paprika and chopped herbs.

Mushroom soup

There is something very comforting about a good mushroom soup, with its particular earthy flavour and smooth richness. Here, garlicky croutons and freshly fried chestnut/cremini mushrooms add flavour and texture to this classic soup.

2 tablespoons sunflower oil
½ onion, chopped
1 leek, trimmed and finely chopped
1 fresh thyme sprig, leaves only
500 g/1 lb. 2 oz. field mushrooms, stalks trimmed and chopped
1 potato, peeled and diced
a splash of Maderia or sherry
700 ml/3 cups good chicken stock
freshly ground nutmeg
1 tablespoon olive oil
200 g/7 oz. chestnut/cremini mushrooms, sliced, to serve
sea salt and black pepper
double/heavy cream, to garnish
chopped fresh chives, to garnish

GARLIC CROÛTONS
2 tablespoons olive oil
1 garlic clove
2 slices of day-old rustic bread, crusts trimmed, cut into cubes

SERVES 4

Heat the sunflower oil in a large saucepan over a medium heat. Add the onion, leek and thyme leaves and fry gently, stirring now and then, for 5 minutes until softened. Add the field mushrooms and fry, stirring, for 3 minutes until lightly browned.

Mix in the diced potato, then add the Madeira or sherry and cook, stirring, for a minute. Pour in the chicken stock and bring to the boil. Reduce the heat, cover and simmer for 25 minutes.

Meanwhile, make the croûtons. Heat the olive oil in a frying pan/skillet over a medium heat. Add the garlic and fry briefly until fragrant. Add the cubes of bread and fry until golden-brown and crisp, discarding the garlic clove when it browns.

Purée the cooked soup until smooth in a food processor or using a handheld stick blender. Season with salt, black pepper and nutmeg. Bring to a simmer again in the pan to heat through.

When ready to serve, heat 1 tablespoon of olive oil in a frying pan over a medium-high heat. Fry the chestnut mushrooms until lightly browned.

Serve the warm soup in bowls, garnished with a swirl of cream, topped with the fried mushrooms and croûtons and and a sprinkle of chopped chives.

Wild mushroom carpaccio

This elegant dish is an easy way to showcase the flavour and texture of wild mushrooms when they are in season. Be sure to use the freshest mushrooms that you can find.

250 g/9 oz. wild mushrooms
1 garlic clove, finely chopped
4 tablespoons extra virgin olive oil
3 tablespoons chopped fresh parsley
12 Parmesan shavings
sea salt and black pepper

SERVES 4

Trim and thinly slice the wild mushrooms. Arrange them in overlapping slices on a serving platter. Season with salt and black pepper.

Sprinkle on the garlic and pour over the olive oil. Top with the parsley and Parmesan shavings and serve at once.

Mushroom & lentil no-meat balls

These no-meatballs aren't pretending to be something they're not, rather they taste like the umami-rich mushrooms, herbs, spices and earthy lentils that they're made from. They're great for everything from salads, to pasta, to appetizers, and play well with both tomato sauces and pestos – giving you plenty of options, such as these meatball sliders.

170 g/1 cup dried green lentils
700–900 ml/3–4 cups water or vegetable stock
olive oil, for frying
1 red onion, finely diced
3 garlic cloves, finely chopped
1 teaspoon dried oregano
¼ teaspoon fennel seeds
2 tablespoons ground chia seeds
140 g/2 cups of mushrooms (chestnut/cremini or portabellini work great for this), roughly chopped
50 g/⅓ cup raw walnuts, roughly chopped
1 tablespoon tomato purée/paste
2 tablespoons oat flour
salt

TO SERVE (OPTIONAL)
seeded rolls
Broccoli Pesto (see page 134)
tomato sauce
rocket/arugula

a baking sheet, lined with baking parchment

MAKES 12–14

In a large saucepan, combine the lentils with the water or vegetable stock (enough to generously cover the lentils). Add a pinch of salt and bring to the boil. Reduce the heat and simmer over a medium-low heat for 20–25 minutes until tender but not mushy. Once cooked, drain.

In a large frying pan/skillet, heat enough olive oil to cover the base of the pan over a medium-high heat. Cook the onion for 4–5 minutes, stirring occasionally, until softened and translucent. Add the garlic, oregano and fennel seeds and season with salt. Cook for another minute until fragrant.

Meanwhile, combine the ground chia seeds with 6 tablespoons water in a small bowl and leave to stand for at least 5 minutes.

In a food processor or blender, combine the cooked lentils, mushrooms, cooked onion mixture, walnuts, tomato purée, chia seeds and oat flour. Process to a rough, slightly chunky dough, scraping down the sides a couple of times.

Preheat the oven to 180°C/160°C fan/350°F/gas 4.

Form the mixture into golf ball-sized balls and arrange close together on the prepared baking sheet. Bake in the preheated oven for 30 minutes until slightly browned and warmed through. Great served as sliders in rolls with pesto, tomato sauce and rocket, if desired.

Portabellini mushrooms with beans & lemon tahini dressing

Portabellini mushrooms have a really lovely, deliciously savoury flavour and are well worth seeking out, but at a pinch, you could use brown chestnut/cremini mushrooms as an alternative if you can't get hold of them.

500 g/18 lb. 2 oz. portabellini mushrooms, stalks removed
100 ml/⅓ cup extra virgin olive oil
2 garlic cloves, finely chopped
1 teaspoon fresh thyme leaves
4 generous handfuls of baby spinach
400-g/14-oz. can cannellini beans, drained and rinsed

LEMON TAHINI DRESSING
75 g/⅓ cup tahini paste
grated zest and juice of 1 lemon
2 garlic cloves, grated

SERVES 3–4

Preheat the oven to 180°C/160°C fan/350°F/gas 4.

Put the mushrooms on a baking sheet. Mix the oil, garlic and thyme together and spoon all but a tablespoon over the mushrooms. Bake for 10–15 minutes until the mushrooms are cooked.

Stir the spinach and beans together with the remaining spoonful of garlic and thyme oil, and spoon this around the cooked mushrooms. Return everything to the oven for 4–5 minutes until the spinach is lightly wilted and the beans are warm.

Arrange everything on a serving platter and pour over any juices that are left in the pan.

Mix all the ingredients for the tahini dressing together in a bowl with 60–75 ml/¼–⅓ cup of water and drizzle over the mushrooms to serve.

Garlic mushrooms & goats' cheese on toast

The rich, earthy taste of mushrooms makes them perfect for this rustic dish. For a quick brunch, garlicky mushrooms are great partnered with soft, creamy goats' cheese. The kind of cheese you are looking for is a soft fresh cheese, not aged, so it will not have a rind.

8 field mushrooms
3 garlic cloves, crushed
3 tablespoons olive oil
25 g/3 tablespoons pine nuts
2 tablespoons balsamic vinegar
4 slices of sourdough bread
150 g/5¼ oz. fresh goats' cheese
sea salt and black pepper
fresh tarragon, to serve

SERVES 3–4

Preheat the oven to 200°C/180°C fan/400°F/gas 6. Put the mushrooms, garlic and oil in a roasting pan. Toss well and season. Roast in the preheated oven for 15 minutes until tender. Stir in the pine nuts and balsamic vinegar halfway through roasting.

Just before the mushrooms are ready, toast the slices of sourdough bread and spread with the goats' cheese. Place the mushrooms on top, stalk-side up, scatter with the tarragon and serve immediately. Add more seasoning, if necessary.

Index

Credits

RECIPE CREDITS

Celia Brooks Brown
Honey-roasted courgettes with feta

Chloe Coker & Jane Montgomery
Beetroot risotto

Megan Davies
Apple & cumin slaw with lime dressing
Apple & kale salad
Blackened romano pepper, tomato & chilli salad
Cayenne roasted sprouts with chickpeas & apricots
Celery waldorf
Chicken & broccoli pasta
Chipotle red pepper soup
Dried mushroom risotto
Greens on toast
Honey, miso & soy aubergine with yogurt & coriander
Leek & cauliflower gratin
Lemon-roasted fennel & dill pasta bake
Maple-roasted celeriac with feta & parsley
Pea & capers on eggy bread
Roasted carrots & legumes with peppercorn & parsley
Roasted marrow & courgetti pasta
Roasted shallots with green yogurt
Whole baked fennel

Ross Dobson
Pickled aubergine
Spaghetti with squash, sage & pecorino
Spinach & chickpea curry

Amy Ruth Finegold
Shaved broccoli & buckwheat salad with dukkah topping

Matt Follas
Artichokes with garlic butter
Aubergine pasta with beans
Broad bean hummus
Caramelized red onion chutney
Carrot & kale juice
Celeriac remoulade
Pea & wasabi dip
Pepper, tomato & celery juice
Pimm's salad
Rainbow chard & comté quiche

Liz Franklin
Carrot tart tatin with ginger & mint yogurt
Charred hispi cabbage with juniper butter & crispy freekeh
Charred turnip & red onion salad
Portabellini mushrooms with beans & lemon tahini dressing
Purple sprouting broccoli & flageolet beans with preserved lemon mayo
Roast butternut squash with lentils, pomegranates & pine nuts
Roasted parsnips cauliflower, cabbage & fennel with green lentils
Roasted red cabbage with charred broccoli, cherries & almonds

Tonia George
Garlic mushrooms & goats' cheese on toast

Lizzie Kamanetzky
Soupe aux Cailloux

Jackie Kearney
Corn cobs with salted chilli olive oil

Jenny Linford
Heritage tomato fennel salad
Greek rice-stuffed tomatoes
Green tomato chutney
Mushroom soup
Spiced red tomato chutney
Spinach tomato soufflé
Summer tomato tart
Wild mushroom carpaccio

Kathy Kordalis
Asparagus & gorgonzola frittata
Asparagus with hollandaise sauce
Avocado & kale grain bowl with tahini-coriander dressing
Braised broad beans & peas with mint & trofie pasta
Corn & quinoa fritters with crispy bacon & beetroot yogurt
Cucumber & herb grain salad
Fregola with courgettes, corn, basil & ricotta
Honeyed heritage carrot & baby beetroot grain platter
Miso & umeboshi baked pumpkin with quick asparagus & carrot kimchi
Pea & olive pistou
Potato & rosemary focaccia
Ratatouille tart with mascarpone, mozzarella & basil
Roasted vegetable & orecchiette salad with tomato & caper dressing
Spiced potatoes in rice pancakes
Simple summer tomato sauce
Warm saffron baby potatoes with lemon & yogurt

Theo A. Michaels
Green vegetable medley
Tray-baked greens

Orlando Murrin
Caeser salad 'green goddess'
Caponata
Cauliflower & cherry tomato bake
Chicken salad with orange, avocado & dates
Creamy orzo with Brussels sprouts & sausages
Gnocchi with peas, mascarpone & black garlic
Ham, spinach & mozzarella galettes
Linguine with porcini, pecorino & marsala
Potato & Smoky Salmon Hash
Red pepper, chorizo & new potato frittata
Risotto primavera
Roast vegetable cassoulet with sizzled artichokes
Seriously cheesy cauliflower
Shakshuka
Spanakopita strudel
Three-mushroom goulash

Louise Pickford
Charred leeks with tarator sauce
Pea & mint soup

James Porter
Cucumber pickles

Fiona Smith
Sprout, cabbage & lettuce sauté

Leah Vanderveldt
Baking tray pizza with pesto winter squash
Blistered tomatoes
Broccoli pesto
Cauliflower steak sandwiches
Farro risotto with green peas
Leek, cauliflower and fennel soup
Mushroom & lentil no-meatballs
Roasted aubergine po'boys with white bean purée & herby slaw
Sweet potato falafel
Thai vegetable curry
Tomato basil salsa
Winter vegetable bowl

Sunil Vijayakar
Cauliflower masala

PICTURE CREDITS

Peter Cassidy
Pages 51, 68, 69, 72, 75, 76, 115, 142 centre, 142 right, 143.

Richard Jung
Pages 104 right, 142 left.

Mowie Kay
Pages 7 top left, 12, 14, 15, 22, 23, 25, 47, 49, 53, 66, 70, 79, 83, 90 left, 90 right, 94, 101, 102, 105, 119, 138, 145, 157, 158, 166.

David Munns
Page 99.

Steve Painter
Pages 3, 4, 7 bottom left, 8 centre, 8 right, 9, 19, 26, 27, 31, 32 right, 33, 50 left, 50 right, 64, 80, 88, 91, 104 left, 104 centre, 110, 116, 118, 128, 129, 132, 133, 153, 160 centre, 172.

Rita Platts
Pages 28, 35, 39, 40, 97, 98, 123, 127, 135, 154, 163.

William Reavell
Pages 2, 6, 90 centre.

Nassima Rothacker
Pages 32 centre, 50 centre, 56, 62, 89.

Kate Whitaker
Pages 32 left, 147.

Clare Winfield
Pages 1, 5, 7 centre right, 8 left, 11, 16, 18, 20, 24, 36, 43, 44, 48, 54, 57, 58, 61, 65, 71, 77, 84, 85, 87, 93, 106, 107, 108, 111, 112, 120, 124, 125, 131, 136, 137, 139, 140, 146, 149, 150, 151, 156, 160 left, 160 right, 161, 164, 165, 167, 168, 171.